BRAVE

The untold true stories of bravery and survival

by

LAUREN-J. COVITO

CONTENTS

Brave

On a late rainy night, I'd take a drive with my father into the city. With my young overactive mind, I feared the harshness with which the rain the fell, the drops falling violently against the metal of the car roof, almost deafening. The ear-splitting raindrops filled my body and my thirsty imagination with an anxious fear. And at the same time, it caused a reverential fear.

I am in awe of life.

Because life means death, and to be dead you didn't need to be roaming lifelessly in the soil of the earth.

Nature is reckless in all its beauty.

With all the patience in the world, I even got to choose the music for the drive, *thanks dad*. At the tender age of thirteen, staring at life through a window, trying to digest the images hastily passing my eyes. Looking out at the now quiet city, listening to the words that always comforted me. I was able to inhale the moment, my surroundings and drown in the silence.
But as silent as the city was, this place I call home held secrets so deep. I could only dig into it with my sensitive imagination.

Creating the depths of a secret. Secrets still too dark for my young mind.

Women in high heels and skin tight dresses. Waving their hands around. The hand in the air an urge for attention, a cry for help or just another day at work. These women chew their gum loudly; my guess was it must have been a nervous habit. Thumbs up as they await the cars to pull over, preparing to give themselves.

I'd express my desire for years to my father about how I needed to speak to a woman who has chosen this walk of life. Whether they have chosen this path, I was desperate for an explanation. My father never held me back. He encouraged me to do it and for years.

I failed.

Already comprehending at that tender age what was about to take place. It's amusingly absurd how the act of sex is easier to understand, how it's one of those things you don't need to experience to understand it. But it takes years and years to know the meaning of intimacy, of love and being in love. Some find it; some will never understand it, or some will never know it.

My young mind filled with thoughts. Thoughts that were clashing with my willingness to understand.

Maybe she has a family to feed.
Surely, she doesn't want this.
How does she give herself to so many faces?
She doesn't know love.

Then I'd ponder on and evaluate the man in the car, with a quick rush of disgust. Only the shape of his silhouette is visible to my curious eyes, the woman on full display but the man behind the scene, buttering her up for a night's work. Only his silhouette, the silhouette of his secret.

The rest of whatever dignity he had left, he was allowed to keep it safe.

He could be married.
What if he is someone's father?
Directions, perhaps he was lost.
He has never known love.

It began. My mind ever growing, hidden secrets unfolding with age yet the core I could not reach.

Growing up in South Africa, my ears were exposed to all kinds of sexual abuse that spread the country.

The news daily covered stories of babies being raped, boys being raped and molested. Where within certain cultures and their beliefs, being a lesbian is a disease and they called their cure: "Corrective Rape."

Rape a cure?

I've heard it all.

At times, I still get nauseous of the race we are, when my disappointment and grief take control of my heart. The immense sadness causes shame to ripple through my skin.

Classified human along with these shadows for men, who come only to steal. If this was human, then human is not what I want to be. Let me be dust blowing in the wind.

These disturbing headlines never left me, a victim abused, a soul tormented for life.

Now at as a married woman at the courageous age of 28. My imagination conjures up an image of human beings lined up. An endless line of lives of all races, all ages. No discrimination. Owned. Ready to be sold, ready to be used then thrown away, labelled.

100% Human.

My sensitivity toward opportunity, toward life, is overwhelming and at times paralyzes my senses. Sadness amplified, concern for things I could never control causes my breathing to become heavy on my chest. Imperfection the truest form of art. Beauty is heavenly, and Love is grace, unmerited favour.

This sensitivity has allowed my mind to transition; it opened to how crazy the world was. How little there was being done for such heinous crimes. How many get away? Who are these soul thieves?

Was the flesh this weak that it needed to become nothing less than monstrous?

It was time to become courageous, to ask the questions burning in my heart. I started the journey. On my journey to filling these pages, pages I could have never filled on my own, stories based on what my imagination thought the reality of a victim was. No, these are stories that were not invented but lived. Eight amazing women share their most profound hurt of being a victim with me, and now reader, with you. With no boundaries, no fear and no pretence.

A dream of mine fulfilled, the dream? Was the knowledge as to what goes on behind those closed doors. The dream was finally asking the questions. Struck with how emotionally unprepared I was regarding the much-awaited insight.

Knowledge never hurt so bad.

The slightest form of understanding has occurred, and this is what my heart believes: Rape, abuse, molestation call it what you want. Levels of rape do not exist. The scars are deep for every victim. Suffering does not discriminate. Abuse is abuse. A deep pain devoted to their souls.

The dream was not to say *I understand*. I could never understand. Nonetheless, these amazing women share the depths of their pain with the world. Exposing the bottomless pits of every secret no mind could fathom. In unfortunate events of suffering choosing a life. You hold in your hand not only a book, or a story but a reality lived.

Read how silence stares bravery dead in the eye. For this moment and every page, be still, be silent. And hear silence breaking, watch bravery unfold with every word. See bravery in the form of a woman.

Brave has a face. Brave has a name. Brave has survived.

These are the untold stories of bravery and survival.

Turning Pages

Matthew:

Hey. I am hearing about a conversation between your nieces Shannon, Amy and their father Jason. Where discussion was held about what I did to you as a kid and that it wasn't the worst thing I had done. I killed my wife. Is this true? And that I passed you around to my friends for money?

Me:

I never said anything about your wife. I know she killed herself because she was *unbalanced.* And as far as what happened to me, I talked to Christie before I found out what she was like because I was concerned about you being with the girls and doing to them what you did to me. As far as what you did to me. I said you sold me to your friends for drugs and molested me on an almost nightly basis. Because you did. You passed me around to Curtis, Chad, Paul and Tyler. For what? So, you could get high?
What would you call it?

Matthew:

Fuck you. I never passed you around for nuthin'. And fuck you for telling anybody. Especially the kids and Julie's ex. I was a dumb kid that was molested and didn't know any better. I tried to apologize years ago, and fuck anyone who thinks I killed Malinda.

Me:

Fuck me? You are the reason I wake up shaking and crying every night. You are the reason I have PTSD and have trouble leaving my house every day. You were molested too, I get that but don't you EVER disrespect me like that again. And don't ever contact me again.

Stepping out onto the patio of my apartment with my pipe in my hand and my earphones in place. Allowing the music to travel into the abyss of my mind and penetrate every nerve of my body. The music preparing to ease and comfort every trace of pain that comes with having fibromyalgia. Exciting my nerves and mind as I help them overcome the rough patches with the cannabis filled vape.

The texts between my brother Matthew and I vivid, it felt as if every word was in front of my eyes, yet the words were not before my eyes. No. The words were engraved into my eyes. The anatomy of my eyes become his words, my words. Our words.

How something that was meant to be so pure, filled with an unconditional love between siblings, was brought to nothing, rotten in so many areas. It's safe to say there was never anything normal about it. I feel my eyebrows lifting slightly, confirming it. Confirming our picture of love had been distorted a long time ago. Like a perfect painting ruined by desperate palms dripping with black paint, a massacre of all things beautiful is its motive as the palms maliciously slide over the masterpiece.

The perfect image was supposed to be our image of love. I know, because I'd once painted it with my very own hands. Colorful. Innocent and warm.

The hurt.
The blackness distorted our masterpiece.

I'm having a down day. A day where my mind aches to remember and forget at the same time. My mind willingly and delicately skillful drowns out the music in my ears. Squinting at the smoke clouds as they become yellow with tinges of green. The yellow clouds take shape, floating on waves of wind forming yellow curtains, possibly from the light filtering through.
But the light was only memories that were surfacing. I am terrified. The curtains now dancing with the wind turn into the sound of turning pages.
First, it's loud in my ears. Then. I see it.

The turning pages loudly became the penthouse magazine the boys were flipping through.

The man next door to my grandparents had two boys and his boys showed us his dad's magazine. Matthew, my brother along with my cousins, Jamie and Scott and I would play with the boys. I remember all of us knowing things about sex that no child our age should know. Only to find out years later that the man had molested my cousin, Jamie. She'd told me so herself. As much as my memory fails to remember the intricate details of those years, I had no doubt of what was happening around me. I am positive, my certainty rooted deep in my gut that my brother was molested as well. Jamie molested me, my brother molested Scott, who was the same age as me. Matthew and Jamie would try to make Scott and I do things to each other.

It's all a vicious cycle of silent suffering.

I am now wholly swallowed by the surfaced memory. Truth is, I honestly felt it was as much my fault as it was theirs and that if anyone were to find out, I would be the one to get into trouble. There is only one way to describe it. I felt trapped.

When my grandfather passed away, I was about seven, my grandmother moved and we never went back there.

The boys and their father's penthouse magazines. The things I'd have to do. The things the man did to us, all left behind.

When I was six, Matthew who is four years older started molesting me at home. He told me all big brothers do this with their sisters to practice. At first, it was just once in a while where I'd play the games he so convincingly got me to play along with, but within a year the game became the game that never ended, it became a habit.

He was my babysitter when my parents worked so I was pretty much at his mercy. Most of the time he was the typical big brother, annoying me by waking me up with heavy metal blasting, doing housework and making sure I do mine (mostly). But at night we shared a bedroom and behind closed doors in the quiet of the night, in the silence that was so loud it would possess my body with fear, he would make me come to his bed.

By the time, I was seven, my brother's friends, Curtis, Chad, Paul, and Tyler would come hang out when my parents were at work and *have fun*. Fun was smoking weed on the back porch and fun was molesting me.

My brother molested me and I didn't like it, but he never made me fear him. It was more like an annoying chore that I couldn't tell anyone about because I would get in trouble too.

His friends scared me. I honestly believe that my brother is the only reason they never raped me. A couple of them would have gone through with it, without second guessing. Mostly they made me give them hand jobs or tried to get me to give them oral. Sometimes they would do stuff to me.

A *normal* day for me was waking up for school, go to school, probably get bullied or teased. Some of my classmates were assholes as if I didn't have enough to deal with. I'd then go home. If my brother's friends were over, I would either just go in and face it or I'd go and find a friend to hang with. Most of my friends had homework or couldn't come out or whatever. And I would end up home again.

The odds were everlastingly against me.

In what seemed a robotic routine, they would pull out the folding bed from the couch and put one of my stepdad's porn VHS tapes. The tapes that every now and then would have static sounds in the background, white lines vaguely appear, apparent signs that it had been used far too much. The images never disappeared and they would never leave me be.

So, they'd make me do things to them and on occasion do things to me.

They would have everything put back by the time my folks got home. Then we would make sure we got our chores done. We would watch TV with our parents till bedtime and then go to bed. After our parents were back to watching TV he would have me come to his bed or he would come to mine, we would have to whisper because sound travelled. If we talked too loud, our stepdad would come up and spank us with a leather belt. And so it went on, at times it felt I lived the same day over and over again. Everyone lived, everyone changed. Not me, I remained the same. I hated being at home.

I was terrified of walking to friends' houses because I would often run into Curtis, who would with his own authority tell me I *owe* him. If I ran into Chad, he would just follow me like a stalker till I reached a friend's house. I was terrified of Curtis because of his threats to rape me, but I was more afraid of Chad because he gave off this 'Quiet psycho' vibe.

There was nowhere I could walk that was safe. I think that more than anything was why I wanted a bike.

By the time I reached twelve, I managed to conjure up the best ways of dealing with my life and I tried to kill myself a few times. Once I took a half a bottle of Tylenol.

I had no concept of what it would take to kill myself, but I wanted it to be clean. No mess.

So, I chose pills. When that didn't work, I tried to set our house on fire with my brother and I in the house. The closest I got to burning down the house was melting parts of the carpet but no fire. The excuse given to my parents was that I had tried to light a candle and it fell. The truth is, I didn't want to live anymore and wanted to take him out with me. But I'd failed.

I gave up after that. I think I just reached a point where I accepted that I would never get away.

This was my reality, my inescapable, foreordained destiny.

At that time, Matthew got involved in stealing neighborhood bikes and got caught.

He spent some time in Juvi. After that, he was sent to live with my biological father a couple states away. We moved that summer into a different part of town.

There was light at the end of the tunnel, my destiny could change, after all. I had convinced my innermost thoughts that we are starting over. I was safe and free from the abuse. Yet the baggage still heavy on my being, I carried it with me in ways I couldn't understand till later.

After failed attempts of taking whatever life it was I was living, the attempts at erasing it. After convincing myself things were turning around.

I turned thirteen just in time for the beginning of Junior High. On my first day, I met two girls who later became my best friends. Jessica and Suzan, who were playing on some folded bleachers and I just clicked with them. We were the *three amigos*. The three of us were pretty much inseparable.

On Valentine's day, our school was having a dance and I wore a denim skirt for the first time. Things were turning around alright, going from my usual attire and approach to clothing which was to hide behind the baggy clothes. A skirt.

My skirt was an inch above the knee, back then that was a miniskirt. I wore a valentine's day sweatshirt with the skirt and got lots of compliments. I felt good.

I had a boyfriend, Alex but I would only kiss then. I was terrified of anything more because of my past. Yes, at the age of thirteen it's safe to say I had a past. He and I would often go on walks around the school campus, sometimes on the trails behind the school track which led into some wooded areas. We went on a walk before the assembly that was kicking off the dance. We went into the woods and he talked me into sitting on a log. He started kissing me and his hands were going everywhere. I froze.

I honestly didn't know how to say "NO".

I couldn't argue. I couldn't fight. I didn't know what to do. I was reliving the abuse all over again, my doomed destiny resurfaced. I was never going to be free. If abuse and pain were two enormous hands, it certainly was wrapped tightly around my neck and all the times I thought it had abandoned me, those hands were always holding my hands.

He got my clothes off and tried to penetrate. He couldn't get "it" in.

"It hurts." I said.
"It's supposed to hurt." He told me.

My mind was racing with what to do, all I could come up with was telling him my friends would miss me at the rally. Only then did he let me up to get dressed. I made it back to the rally to see Suzan and Jessica perform in the cheer squad. I went to the dance and pretended nothing happened. The enormous hands of pain had shut my mouth.

A day or two later I told Suzan and Jessica what happened. I didn't know it was rape. I had no idea why I felt so angry and so dirty. Jessica, as far as I know never told anyone. Suzan however, told the school gossip, one of the girls who was a notorious bully, she had told everyone in the school, sometimes right in front of me, that I had sex with Alex in the woods and like a bullet to the chest, it hurt. I became suicidal and destructive. I would run out of classrooms and slam the door. I still didn't have a great grasp of how to kill myself, so this time I took an entire box of Vivarin.

It made me sick but nothing more. This complicated thing we call life had a hold of me. And it wasn't ready to let go.

One day at school I saw Alex walking to class, I snapped and everything went black. I found my hands around his throat and he was turning blue. It was like everything was happening to someone else.

I could hear giggling and all I could do was squeeze.

Three ninth graders had to pull me off of him and I realized the giggling was coming from me, in that moment I was alone with my mind, immersed, drowning in every emotion my body could hold. Destruction became me in that moment.

I went to the office and talked to the councilor. I told her what happened and how I felt, and she told me it was rape. I still didn't believe her. I wore a skirt, I didn't say no, I didn't fight, how could it be rape? I confessed my suicide attempts and she contacted my mom. I had to break it to my mom what happened and my hesitation to call it rape, but she assured me that it was and it wasn't my fault. He went away.

I don't know if things happened behind closed doors to get him out or if he just happened to transfer out due to coincidence. Only to find out later, that he was kicked out of my school because my mom threatened legal action against the school if they didn't remove him.

A few months after everything that had gone on Matthew came back home. We were sitting on the couch and he asked me if he could go down on me. Nauseated, I couldn't even look at him. Taking the longest blink, I just closed my eyes. Exhaled. And said.

"No."

"Okay." He replied and never tried to touch me again. That was my first time of understanding the power of "No". From that moment on, he was my big brother. Not my abuser, not my molester. My brother. I would talk to him about everything. I would go to parties with him and he would keep me safe. I wanted to believe it was all over and physically it was, but emotionally and mentally, it was only beginning.

Surviving the physical parts was easy.

When you aren't afraid to die, pain is just pain, it will either end or it won't. And death, death was always on the table for me.

But the anger. Rage. Self-doubt. Self-blame. Self-destruction. They last for decades.
They don't decompose and become one with the Earth.
They seep in under your skin.
They flow through your veins.
They become you.

I became very promiscuous in Junior High and High school. Seeing as this corruption wouldn't leave me alone, I thought that was all I was good for.
...

I manage a slight smile as I see myself as a child. I remember being a creative child. In most things, fearless. I taught one of my younger cousins to read and write, and I loved music.
I was never particularly good at any one thing, but I had many creative interests. I never kept a diary as I was always paranoid someone would read it. As a teen, I changed looks kind of often, always trying to find my place I guess.

My hair has been many different colors from black to purple to very blonde to red. (I still haven't done blue... life goals).

I went crazy a few times, lost the plot. I think everyone around me chalked my odd behaviour up to teenage hormones or whatever, but I had gone straight up loopy a couple of times. Once I believed a vampire was coming for me, this time I didn't say no.

I wanted him to come for me, to hunt me down and take me wherever he was going.

Once I was convinced my brother's ex (who was out of the picture for a couple years by this time) was stalking me to get to him. To be fair, she did do that when she was still in the picture, but this was long after that.

There is one good memory peeping through the yellow curtain of smoke clouds. (Laughing). I remember once when my parents finally split my brother and I moved up into separate rooms, they'd sleep on the folding bed. It was another night of them being gone.

I swear they didn't go out all the time, that's just when the big shit happens. So, one night my brother and I were playing a sort of game where we would sneak into the other's bedroom and try to scare each other.

This had been going on for a little while and I had a brilliant idea. I had one of those big Barbie heads they sold, the ones where you could style their hair and put makeup on them. My memory recalls me having very blonde hair as a child, so I grabbed the Barbie head, shoved it in one of my flannel nightgowns and laid it on my bed with some clothes stuffed in it for realism then laid it on its side with its back to the door.

I then went and stood behind the door and waited. Sure enough, it slowly opened up and I saw his silhouette creep to my bed. He tried to scare the dummy just as I jumped out behind him. He screamed a high-pitched shriek and ran to his room slamming the door. I laughed all night over that.

The corners of my mouth completely creased now. All good things feel as if they are just for a moment as I feel my chest jump, I exhale a smile and in an instant, my mouth closes and I inhale one of my worst memories, the only time my brother physically hurt me.

We were home alone, folks were at the movies or dinner or something. He told me he wanted to try something, so he got out the Vaseline and bent me over.

He pushed into my back and I screamed from the pain. He immediately pulled out and I ran to the bathroom locking the door. He sat outside the door for hours trying to apologize and get me to come out. I just sat hugging my knees and cried the entire time. The image, my masterpiece of love at this point was beyond distorted. It was destroyed.

When I was seventeen, I was riding with a couple friends and I was *riding shotgun*. We drove past Alex's house and I pointed it out to them. I closed my eyes and suddenly I was there, watching it happen all over again. I saw myself on the grass with my very first stupid denim skirt. Alex assuring me it was meant to hurt.
The cheer squad about to commence.
Suffocating on the word *no*. The word that would not come out of my mouth. The 17-year-old me watched the younger me. I felt the air of the moment on my skin, over the surface of my eye and through my eyelashes as I blink.
When it was over, I opened my eyes and the car was pulled on the side of the road and my friends were trying to wake me up. I had shut down mid-sentence and was non-responsive, still breathing an active pulse but completely out. Until I started crying because I finally understood the truth that it was rape.

I was raped.

It wasn't my fault. It was the first big step in my healing. The next big one doesn't happen for a few more decades, but that was when I started healing from the rape.

I'd then survived living with a narcissistic mother and daughter. Margaret and Shelly, who only fanned the flames of my insecurities. I lived with them for eight years because I thought Shelly and I were in love. It wasn't love, it was obsession, jealousy and it was manipulation. Shelly was only the gasoline on the flames of the fire. The manipulation and jealousy were not enough, the flames weren't high enough. There were many occasions where she would make out with other women in front of me and then expected me to be ok with it, even though we still shared the same bed. Unfortunately, I was so brainwashed by then I blamed myself. The thoughts consistent, repetitive. Making me dizzy.

If I cleaned a little more.
If I worked a little harder.
Things would get better.

If I clean a little more.
If I worked a little harder.
Things would be better.

Things would be better.

Of course, it didn't. When I lived with Margaret and Shelly becoming sober was impossible. If I quit drinking, I was bullied into drinking "with the family" but if I drank, I drank *too much*, there was no winning solution because moderate drinking wasn't in my skillset. Towards the end of my drinking, I didn't drink to feel good or be happy, I drank to not feel and to pass out at night. I drank for the exhilarating thrill of being numb.

By the time I quit, I was going to bed with a twelve pack of beer, getting up the next morning and picking up another twelve pack. I tried quitting many times over the years and always relapsed. Starting out a happy drunk, loud, annoying, telling everyone and some inanimate objects that I loved them.

"I love you". Eyes fading and lips puckered on the *you*.

I was lucky though, I had a couple friends who I always partied with who always got me home safe and sound.

As far as I am aware, I've only ever blacked out once. At my friend Yvette's apartment for a get-together. Yvette had gotten me a bottle of *Captain Morgan's Spiced Rum*, private stock for either my birthday or for Christmas, I can't remember. In any case, I had made myself a couple rum and cokes and was feeling pretty good, had a nice buzz going.

Trevor, Yvette's friend, poured me a very tall shooter (think tall shot glass). I told him I didn't drink straight booze. He looked me in the eye, "Wuss". That got my hackles up and I squared my shoulders in defiance and took the shot. After that I was no longer drinking with booze in mind. All I could process was that I was thirsty and, "Oh, look."
A tall glass of liquid (because Trevor kept refilling it) was sitting in front of me. I must have ended up drinking half the entire bottle. One moment I was sitting at Yvette's computer playing with her music and the next I woke up on the couch with no pants on and wet hair.

Apparently, I had walked into the bathroom, collapsed near the toilet and lost a number of bodily fluids all over the floor no blood, but everything else. Yvette found me and yelled at Trevor, "You did this to her, you clean it up."

Distant echoes of his voice telling me that they had to take my pants off to wash them, and I remember the shower hosing me down as I lay in the tub. I tried to quit drinking after that, but I was still living with Margaret and Shelly at the time so that lasted a couple weeks before I was drinking again. To this day, the smell of rum makes me queasy. Slightly causing me to scrunch my nose.

I take another puff from my vape.

The day I left, I can only describe it as a divine intervention. Hecate. Margaret was in my face screaming at me. I was filled with a massive instinct to push her away, my reaction would've normally been fight or flight, but then I suddenly felt a calm wash over me. I found myself responding to her accusations with calm and rational answers which only pissed her off more. She told me to get out. She meant the room, I took it otherwise.

I went and packed a bag with my work clothes and necessities, called a friend to come get me and left.

It took me a few months to get back on my feet and I never moved back. Margaret and Shelly were only trains passing by the station of my life.

The last time I quit, I was living with a friend while I looked for an apartment. I had come home one night drunk after doing Karaoke with a couple friends and went to bed. That night I had a dream of my life ten years down the road. My relationship with my family, including my daughter, a dream so real, so horrific that when I woke up, I said: "I'm done". I stopped buying alcohol and it hasn't been allowed in my house since. I did allow friends to bring alcohol over once, but the rule was that if they brought it over, they had to take it home. I didn't want any left behind because the temptation is still kinda strong sometimes

Eight months after I left Margaret and Shelly and was back on my feet, I found a job working in a CD/DVD store and a woman came up to me and asked me if we had Pink Floyd *The Wall* on DVD. I said, "yes" and walked over to where I knew we had the copy.

I handed it to her and she held it up to someone standing behind me and said, "See Curtis, I told you they had it."

I turned around and standing in front of me was Curtis, the very man (boy at that time) who would tell me I *owed* him and who abused me for so many years was in the store.

I don't know if he recognized me, my once long blonde hair was black and short, and I had gotten chubbier than when I was a kid. But I must have gone several shades paler because all I could say was "Excuse me." then walked over to my co-worker and asked him to take over the sale. I went straight into the back room and closed the door. I called a good friend and she helped me calm down. My co-worker let me know when they had gone and told me to take my time to come back out. If Mark (my husband, boyfriend at the time) hadn't been picking me up that night, I would have ended up in a bar getting tanked. I was six months sober by then. He drove me home, all I could offer him was silence, I could barely talk.

We got home and I just collapsed in his arms. The two enormous hands that suffocated me with pain, they had lost. I surrendered to the pain, I let it come up, I rode it out. Mark held me through all of it.

That was the moment I knew I couldn't go through it alone anymore. I got into recovery groups and it helped me learn how to function without alcohol.

So many times, too many times I've made excuses for why my brother did what he did. I blamed the drugs he was doing, I blamed the fact that he was molested too, I blamed his friends. I told myself he was different, that he was changed. Until one day we were at a bar with my brother, sister-in-law and a few of their friends, for some karaoke. My brother was telling me how he and his friends have group sex with his wife. I realized then that he hadn't changed he just replaced his sister with his wife. It was kind of a wake-up call for me and really made me examine our relationship. That was when I finally came to realize how much in denial I was. I stopped talking to him after that.

I've been in and out of therapy over the years, been on many a cocktail of prescription pills and still had mental breakdowns. My biggest saving grace has been the people in my life. I have been married twice, my first when I was twenty-one and I had his daughter. He got custody of her when I lost my home and was couch hopping to stay safe.

My second when I was thirty-two. I'm still married (ten years in a few days of writing this) and we have an amazing little boy who is on the autism spectrum. I can't afford the therapy I need because in America right now, insurance is bullshit. Mine will allow me to have all the access to all the therapy I want... IF we can come up with a $3000 deductible.

Might as well be a million.

It's been a rocky road filled with land mines, potholes and logs on the road. But because of all of that, I was able to recognize and appreciate real kindness when it was shown to me and compassion. Over the years and sometimes as a result of bad relationships, I have made connections with some pretty spectacular people who have helped me on my journey to healing my heart and soul.

The way it's affected me the most is how I see myself and the ability to trust others. I saw myself as an object not worthy of happiness. I kept everyone at arm's length, never really letting them in. It affected how I carried myself, how I dressed, what I did.

As far as love goes, I don't think I ever gave up on the idea. I love my parents, I love my brother, I love my children, I love my friends, my family, I love anyone who has suffered, I love. I never stopped. But that's the thing about love.

It wouldn't hurt as bad if it wasn't love.

...

"I know you probably never want to hear from me, but I really hope you read this all the way through before deciding. The past couple years have been one of the hardest lessons, pain, and growth. I've learned more about myself than I had known my entire life. I realized that I too had suppressed memories and they've been surfacing. Maybe my brain thinks I'm ready, maybe I've just finally lost what was left of my mind and have no choice. I don't know anymore. I go for a while being ok, and then in a matter of days or hours I can fall down the rabbit hole and it's a hurricane in my head. Memories, emotions, all swirling around and round making me dizzy.
Sorry, rambling. Haven't slept more than a couple hours a night for the last week.

I started to remember. I didn't think it was possible to have blocked anything out because what I did remember was so bad, I didn't think it could have gotten worse.

I remembered our cousins being involved. I remembered Scott being a target, and I remembered Jamie being an instigator. I have never blocked out what you or your friends did to me, but apparently, I blocked out everyone else. What the fuck happened to our family? Was all that because of the man who lived next to Grandma? I remembered that I was abused, but I had you. You were abused and had no one. I can't imagine what that must have been like for you. I imagine you felt betrayed when you found out I told. Please know that the only reason I came out about it in the first place was because I was trying to protect my daughter, and I had no other way to get mom to understand why I didn't want her around you. I had no way of knowing if you would hurt her or if the abuse stopped with me. It was a choice you or my daughter and my children will always come first no matter what. Once I did come out about it, it became an issue of healing.

I remembered when you were my ear and I could talk to you about anything. I remembered when you were my hero.

I remembered how you never intentionally hurt me. I remembered that you were probably the only thing that protected me from Curtis and Chad's brutality. Curtis would threaten to rape me whenever I saw him in the neighborhood, telling me "I owe him". Chad was a stalker psycho. I also realized why I couldn't forgive you. It was because I couldn't forgive myself. I have nightmares about it. It has been the main cause of my PTSD. Ultimately, however, I had to admit to myself that I enjoyed a lot of what you did to me. It was a hard truth to come to and the main reason I had never been able to move on. I didn't like all of it, but some. Your friends were evil and I will never forgive them, but for what it's worth. I do forgive you. I will maintain my distance, I am not trying to make things worse for anyone. I just wanted you to know that I'm sorry. I'm sorry it took so long for me to reach this place, I'm sorry it happened to us at all.
I love you."

Laura

The Lost Diary

Dear new diary. Dear first page. Dear bold line.

New diary, before I scribble all over you and vigorously share my joy. I say vigorously only because at times when I can't withhold my excitement and need of expression my pen tends to move faster than I can think. I'll entrust my heart to you in a moment, it is only vital you know there was a diary before you, another diary I held close to me with pages that comforted me. Pages that absorbed the ink with care as if though it felt everything I was feeling, every emotion seeped through the ink.

The diary where I delicately expressed my hurt. That diary is now long gone; it held too much you see. So, it was taken from me and I wish ... I wish I could have my old diary back just to see what I had written, but it's all gone.

They never told me they would keep it. Therefore, I expected to get it back. I felt a deep sense of loss because it held my personal thoughts and if I hadn't said it enough I'd say it again.

It was my comfort.

Please, my intention is not to make you feel unworthy of my joy and pain. Instead, I'll tell you all about the lost diary; I'll tell you everything it knew and who they were.

Then perhaps you too will soak in my pain and joy. My new friend and new found comfort, this is my story.

Blank page. Bold lines. Inspire my hands.

Many people look back on their childhood and see happy memories. Images of heads thrown back in laughter, of that one boy you'll never forget. You know, the one who'd cause an infinite amount of butterflies to fly wildly in your belly. Unfortunately, I haven't had that luxury growing up. My earliest memories go back to my kindergarten self; these memories consist of hiding behind the couch, crying, waiting with a heaviness on my heart for my parents to stop screaming at each other. The screaming mainly took place in my presence, sometimes behind closed doors, but we, my sister Rachel and I could still hear the stubborn roaring.

We'd both be in tears and for most of the arguments, feel extremely uncomfortable. With every argument so loud it often seemed unclear what they were arguing about in the first place. Eventually, my dad moved into the spare bedroom, giving us a break. For a while, the fighting lessened but started back up again. Nothing changed.

A family stuck in reverse.

A reality for you dearest bold line, my mother and father, they were never a good match from the start. I had learned from an early age that nothing was forever. My dad always manipulated my mom into feeling sorry for him, he had outbursts of severe depression and was a narcissist.

My father didn't even want another kid after my sister was born. To add to the burden he already was my father then also quit his job after we moved to Texas and worked on starting his own business, but nothing ever came from the endless hours he spent cooped up in his office 'working' as he'd call it. Whereas on the other hand, mom worked late hours at a corporate job travelling all the time to support us, she has always been the breadwinner in my family and supported my unemployed father during most of their marriage.

Texas for a moment seemed like an unlucky charm when dad and I got into a car crash right after we moved to Texas; he had developed back problems. Another reason for him to continually mooch off my mom and let her carry all the responsibilities even after his back problems minimalized.

When I was in Kindergarten, my parents filed for divorce and the idea of, 'forever' was forever lost. The entire process was very messy and emotionally draining.

For as long as I can remember, my father and I never seemed to see eye to eye. I've always been a carbon copy of my mother. There's nothing she has that I don't. I stand up for what I believe in and don't take crap from anyone. My mom and I are independent, strong willed and abnormally sarcastic as a matter of fact that often got me into loads of trouble. We are both leaders and like to control our lives. And that, dear diary was a touch of pride and joy all at once.

Allow me to continue; my mother is a great wonder, why not share it with you?

My mother, may almost be 54, but she looks 40. Let's hope I manage to have that in common with her too. Her face barely holds any wrinkles, except for a few crows feet lines fighting for her attention. Her eyes are blue just like mine. Her laugh is very light and airy. At 54 she's rocking a short bob and has only a few grey hairs.

Dearest ink flowing from my pen, draining my memory onto paper allow me this moment. For this is not merely just a memory, it is reality. My mother, she is the strongest person I know. Everything that life has hit her with, she overcame, she pushed through. She's been a single mom since I was in Kindergarten and up to this day is very involved in my life. She made sure to bring me to every practice, that I was always at rehearsal on time, fed and clothed me.

She'd work all day and then even after a long day she'd come home and make me laugh and smile. Her cares vanished, those long hours hardly expressed, selfless in every action. A shoulder to cry on, nurturing advice I would receive, whether I wanted it or not.

If I may express my heart, if there was a speck of love for me floating in my father's heart, being so much like my mother must have caused it to fade away. It pissed my father off to no end. Therefore, I knew there could be no love in his heart for me.

He made it glaringly obvious that I wasn't wanted. He saw my older sister as someone who could do nothing wrong and I was just the devil child who he had to tolerate. Because whether he liked it or not.

I was around. I am around. I will forever by blood be his daughter.

Since the day of my birth, it was evident I was not the apple of his eye, I wasn't even worthy enough to share some of the attention. My mom would often tell me about how I used to cry as a baby and wouldn't calm down unless my mom held me, but continued to cry if my father tried to hold me and calm me down. Our mother-daughter relationship and the pure connection was made to be.

It's no surprise I turned out to be so much like my mother and my sister so much like my father. When we would go to my dad's house, my sister would do everything he asked. I was not like that. When he asked us to clean his entire house, one that we only visited six or so days a month, I would always complain that he saved the dirty work for us when we barely lived there. He didn't like how often I spoke my mind.

Compared to my shy sister, I am way more outgoing we couldn't be more diverse. Rachel is a pale freckled redhead who burns as soon as she steps outside. I have blonde hair and can get some kind of a tan. I've never had trouble making friends. Rachel had one or two friends and at times had trouble making and perhaps keeping them. I'm athletic and interested in theatre; she sticks to art and painting. Complete opposites but sisters nonetheless.

To add to burdensome bricks of hurt stacked on my heart, everything my conscience told me about my father, proved me right. As I later found out my dad didn't even want another child after my older sister was born and was furious when he discovered my mom was pregnant with me.

So needless to say, our relationship was tense, undesired.

After legal fee's depleted and the little savings my father had left, we were forced to move from apartment to apartment with our quality of life decreasing with each move. Most apartments were bug infested; the cops became regulars, and I feared walking my dog alone. Rachel and I shared a small uncomfortable futon. I remember waking up almost every morning with a crick in my neck because the futon was so stiff. Everything in his house was a different shade of brown. It smelled like dog because of our family dog Peanut. *Thanks a lot, Peanut.* I chose Peanut and she was a great dog good company too. My dad got rid of her after I stopped going to his house and didn't even bother to tell me.

Peanut too was not forever.

Things financially got so bad that we got our food from a food pantry. The few clothes my father purchased for me were from thrift stores and Dollar General. Luckily, I only endured this at my father's house and lived quite comfortably at my mom's.

After a while comfort started showing up on my dad's side too. Somehow, my father found a real house for my sister and I to live in; things started looking up for all of us, moving in a better direction. What I enjoyed the most was that we had cable TV. We hadn't had cable since my dad first moved out.

Then there was also the benefit that Rachel and I no longer shared a futon and instead, each had a twin bed. There was a backyard we could do things in, something we hadn't had in a while. It wasn't in a sketchy neighborhood and I felt comfortable going outside and playing. Too bad Peanut would never be able to have enjoyed it with me. The furniture was also nicer than anything we had at his previous apartments. On the surface, it seemed life started showing us mercy.

The only catch was that with all the charming things we now had we shared the house with a roommate. He was a middle-aged man who seemed nice, when you're a child you're usually sensitive to people's exteriors, there was none of that.

No weird feeling, I was pretty comfortable.

He had brown-grey hair, blue eyes, and was severely balding. The loss of hair on his head was so severe, he almost only had hair on the sides of his head and none at the top. He had a moustache and a little bit of scruff for a beard. He also had deep forehead wrinkles and crow's feet. As a third grader, anyone would come across tall, but he wasn't tall at all and also was an average weight.

Josh. That was his name. Josh

So, when I was in third grade, we moved in and there were no complaints. Then for a moment, it got better. Life appeared to have a positive outlook, so positive that after a short amount of time living in this house, we seemed to have money to spare. My sister and I started receiving an allowance, something I'd never had in my entire life. The memories of what I'd spend my allowance on is vague; I do however remember buying soda, yes soda. When we went to the store we never bought any to have at home, the only soda at home was my Dad's favorite Diet-Coke, which we weren't allowed to have.

The roommate, Josh, sincerely he was very friendly. He always brought popcorn home for my sister and I to enjoy. Josh even rented movies on demand for us to watch together. Movies on demand was a luxury considering we hadn't had cable at my father's house in years. And this became a habit, watching movies. It never got tiring. Movies all the time. Every movie a new fantasy to take part in, a new emotion to experience and adventures that blew my mind.

Now we had cable and an infinite amount of movies to watch. Eventually, my dad started to leave my sister and I alone with Josh while he sat in his office on his computer.

One night, my sister, Josh, and I sat down to watch My Sisters, Keeper. Rachel sat on the loveseat in the corner of the room, and Josh and I shared the couch. I was lying down with my legs stretched out along the couch with a blanket on top of them. Sometime during the movie, Josh began to rub my legs gently. I didn't know this at the time, but the slow movement of his hand was very inappropriate. His hand inched its way up to the top of my thighs and continued to caress my legs sensually. He moved his hand further and further into the center of my legs. Staring blankly at the TV, the movie no longer made any sense. Neither was I capable of making any sense of what was happening.

Diary. Bold lines. Is the ink seeping in fast enough? Are you seeing it? Can you feel it?

I was unable to make sense of it all and began to feel very uncomfortable and tried to ignore the sinking feeling in my chest, a sinking so overwhelming I felt frozen and helpless.

Unsure of what to do, I allowed this to continue throughout the rest of the movie. I was only in third grade and didn't know anything about sexual gestures. I wasn't even close enough to my father to distinguish the difference of a gentle, caring caress until Josh placed his hands too far up. A third grader forced to learn the cruel, immoral and dark side of affection.

To this day, I can't watch that movie without feeling sick.

After the horrific encounter, I began to avoid Josh, but he continued to find times to rub my legs, as I sat back doing nothing. I remember him acting like nothing happened, everything was alright, just fine.

Never. Never could I have imagined that it would get worse. For the first few months that we lived with Josh, my dad wouldn't run errands without taking us with him. As everyone got more comfortable with our living situation, my dad started to leave the house without making us come along. One night, my sister had volleyball practice. Volleyball practice was something I despised because it was so annoying. All I had to do was sit there watching the ball glide through the air. In my state of boredom, I would take a spare volleyball and hit it around sometimes. Or invent games only my mind knew how to play. I think Gameboy/ Nintendo DS's were popular during this time so I might have played one. Sometimes I messed around in the bleachers during her practice and went behind them.

Volleyball wasn't my thing, much less was watching it, spending two hours watching other people play volleyball was not how I wanted to spend my nights. Most times I had no choice. Volleyball it was. Bleachers, Nintendo and my imagination, saved me.

Luckily, on this particular night, my father let me stay home. Josh and I sat down to watch a movie, as we always did. I can't recall the exact movie, but it had something to do with aliens. Josh sat on the couch, and I sat on the loveseat. There was no time for me to get into the movie, no peace for my young body, no enjoyment in trying to figure out what the aliens were going to do. Even though we all know aliens either come to destroy earth or in rare Hollywood movies, help earth.

No peace.

I didn't get to watch much of the movie until Josh began to make his move. Josh crept over to where I was sitting and began to push my legs apart. I fought, I tried to resist his advances. The lump in my throat got bigger and bigger until I couldn't even make out a word. I was alone with Josh for the first time and had no clue what was about to happen. He continued to rub my legs and pull at the band of my shorts. By now his body was towering over me and had me pinned down spread eagle. In my head, far off in the depths of my mind, I was screaming, but nothing came out. Even if I had been able to scream, it was useless because we were alone.

His hand eventually made it inside my shorts, and he did things no grown man should ever do to a child. Silent tears rolled down my cheeks.

His evil and demented grin will never escape my mind; it has been etched into my mind.

Forever was good for something, it was good for holding pain.

Luckily, it didn't last long, and I finally broke out from under him. I ran to the room that my sister and I shared, slammed the door and broke out into sobs. Every part of me felt dirty and gross. Sitting, leaning against the door in fear that he would barge in and do something worse. He knocked on the outside of the door telling me that he did *nothing wrong*. I may have been young, but I knew in my heart that he was lying. He kept apologizing and asking me to come out and finish the movie. Not budging from my spot against the door, my fear released with every tear that fell, knowing he was bigger and stronger than I was. If he wanted something more, it wouldn't take him much.

During this time, I kept a diary about my life. The lost diary. I wrote down what Josh did to me. I'm not sure why I did this, but it was almost relaxing. It was like I was telling someone without the consequences of what I had revealed. My back still firmly against the door waiting for my father and sister to return. Until they finally did. Was I going to say something?

For months, I kept the secret of what Josh did to me. It slowly devoured my insides. I walked around the house acting like everything was fine. The horror and hurt, his hands, my fear and sunken chest. Playing on repeat, my young mind analyzing everything. To this day, it's what I do now whenever anything bad happens. Every bad thing becomes a movie on loop and I become the critic.

Diary? Are you wondering why I hadn't told my sister?

Well, I was scared my sister would hate me for ruining our living situation. It did come out, I honestly don't know why I told in the first place. Eventually, I couldn't take it anymore.

...

When I was younger, mom hosted Christmas parties every year. They were pretty fun, with a distinct separation between adults and kids but my mom tried to combine the two groups every so often. Christmas parties also meant that I always had to meet a lot of adults from different sides of the family and some occasional co-workers. All our friends and local family came to our house to celebrate. We had games, dinner and karaoke to keep everyone entertained. My best friend Michael and his sister Sarah were there, and we spent most of the party hanging out in my room. For some reason, I felt compelled to share my secret with them.

Not on paper, but in words. I pulled out my diary and had Michael read the entry from that horrible day. He passed the diary to his sister, whom I was also very close to. Looking back on that day now, it was a very intense secret to tell my young friends. They urged me to tell my mom. I waited until after the party was over to share my secret. I didn't want to ruin my mother's night.

Until I built up the courage and finally, I told her. We were sitting in the living room on the couch with my mom when I told her. My story was told through tears, showers, waterfalls of tears as I cried telling her. My strong and courageous mother, she fought her tears, rubbing my back to calm me down and gave me and endless hug. This hug was certainly forever.
She was so upset; my heart broke all over again. My mother called the police and began the legal process of reporting sexual abuse. The next day, we contacted my father so that we could tell him what had happened. His response was not what I expected. My father didn't seem to believe that anything happened between Josh and me at all. He was convinced that I made the entire thing up. I, a third grader, made up an instance of sexual assault, invented with words from the core of my heart, such filth. Here is your reason for why I didn't want to tell my sister. She did end up siding with my father for a while and not believing me, saying I was ruining everything.

Mentally, I'd like to think this was mainly due to his influence.

I felt betrayed by my dad. Family is always suppose to be there for you. He also put me in that situation with Josh, so part of me blamed him for leaving me alone with a stranger. He was always in his office and left us alone with Josh too many times. I knew we didn't have the best relationship, but in this circumstance, I expected too much. For support from my father, a part of my family to support me through the rough times. He kept insisting that I was trying to ruin his life.

We finally lived in a nice house and had money to spare, but I was trying to take it all away. His words hurt worse than anything Josh did to me.

Josh denied everything from the beginning, and I was forced to continue living in the same house with him. Crying at the thought of going to my dad's house for the weekend. The only rules placed upon my visit at my dad's house was that Josh was not to be alone in the room with me. This was not followed. I saw him everywhere in the house and spent most weekends cooped up in my room. I couldn't enjoy movies and popcorn at my dad's house anymore. It could not be the same, and our relationship only grew in tension. My father made no effort to prevent Josh from hanging around me.

My family has attended therapy ever since the divorce, and this new situation prompted even more, sessions. The sessions involved uncomfortable couches.

Awkward tension. Forced communication.

My father constantly argued with the therapists, my time in these sessions was spent sitting silently on the couch fighting back tears. The therapists constantly tried to put words in my mouth. When my mom would try, and defend me, it would only intensify my father's anger. He usually put me down and called me manipulative and selfish during most of the sessions. Therapy didn't seem to help our relationship.

I also started attending group therapy at the Children's Advocacy Center. They are a non-profit organization that helps in child abuse investigations. They work alongside Child Protective Services and prosecutors to assist the victims of child abuse. I talked to countless people at the center, repeating my story until I was numb.

Group therapy sessions helped me heal the most. We usually began by talking about our day. Then the conversation might be prompted by the therapist to talk about our abuse and how it affected us. Sometimes that would come up naturally.

There were several couches in the room and we would all sprawl out across them in odd ways.

Sometimes we would all come out crying from how intense the conversations got. Other times we would have light conversations and laugh and be the kids we still were.

During this period I met some of the strongest girls I have ever met. Each of us had a story to tell, a suffering we had to share. We met once a week to discuss our issues and help each other heal. Most of the girls in my group were rape victims.

I had only had a man touch me in my privates.

Sometimes I compared my situation to theirs. They had more supportive family members but suffered more abuse than I did. My mom told me the other day that the social worker on my case asked my mom why she was pushing so hard for my case when it *wasn't that bad.*

Those girls were my support system. Slowly, I started picking up the pieces of my shattered life. They soon added individual therapy to my treatment plan. My therapist was very nice and helped me work through my issues. Eventually, I graduated from group therapy. There was a giant wall outside the therapy rooms with blankets and stuffed animals on shelves. When you completed a milestone in therapy, you could pick out something.

On one occasion, I picked out a lion stuffed animal that sits in my room still to this day. I also received a zebra print blanket that I'll never get rid of. Each of the girls picked a color of sand, assigned a trait that they liked about me to that color, and filled a jar with each layer of sand. *The jar sits on my desk at home, and I'll never get rid of it.*

During my time at the Children's Advocacy Center, my father was not allowed to continue visitation at Josh's home. Instead, we met at a local park every Thursday night for visitation. Rain or shine, we sat at the picnic table.

Father had stark white hair for as long as I can remember. He wore glasses with thin frames, bifocals. His face was very wrinkled. Many people mistook him for my grandfather. He had blue eyes just like my mom, sister, and I. One of his eyes is glass because of an accident that caused him to lose an eye. He always wore formal button downs with khaki/ beige pants. He wore the same plain brown shoes often. I wanted his attention at first because what daughter doesn't, but soon it went away. A small part of me still gets sad when he can't even be bothered to say happy birthday. He had given my sister Christmas gifts for years, and I've received nothing. I know gifts aren't important, but it hurts when he shows her he cares but can't be bothered to do anything for me.

Our dinner included peanut butter and jelly sandwiches with lukewarm lemonade. Sometimes, we played simple card games. Other times, my dad would push me to admit that I was lying about the entire situation. Those were the worst nights.

On a bad visit. He would bring up my abuse, how he missed the house, anything to make me feel bad. Or, at times I was already in a bad mood and avoided any questions, there were times I didn't want to talk at all about anything, causing him to get mad. Sometimes I would complain because he wouldn't interact with us and then he would go on a tangent about how he had a long day and was tired, and I was a brat.

On a good day. We would play various card games to pass the time and not talk much. Sometimes my sister and I played on the playground and not a word would be spoken.

A rollercoaster of emotions, at times there was a hint of happiness and at times I would sit at the picnic table crying, counting down the minutes until I could return home. My mom reluctantly sent us to that park every Thursday, watching how upset we were after each visit. My father insisted he was looking for another place to live and that this situation was only temporary.

That spring break, my father decided to take us camping. He took us back to the house where my abuse occurred and had us sit in the car while he grabbed some supplies that he forgot. Just seeing the outside of that house brought back my anxiety. The palms of my hands sweating, my breathing increased, and my heart hardened. My biggest fear was spending a week in a camper with my sister and dad. We didn't have wifi; this was before everyone had an iPhone and I only had an iPod to play with. The campsite we went to went to only had porta potties, a fact I was not excited about. We also didn't have a shower, so I wasn't looking forward to that as well.

I survived both the camp and my fears.

When my mom found out that he had taken us back to that house despite being ordered not to, she was furious. My mother drove to my sister and I and took us to stay in a hotel for the week. She ignored all of my father's calls and refused to return us to his care. This wasn't legally allowed, but my mom didn't care. She later told me that she was so mad she didn't even think of the consequences. I was so grateful that she saved me from another uncomfortable spring break with my dad. She possibly even saved me from another encounter with Josh. From this moment on, visitation with my dad was on hold. I was the one who told my mom that we had visited Josh's house, so therefore my father was furious with me yet again.

Soon, he found another house to live in. Visitation started again, but we continued to meet at the park because the new house was far away. More dreadful Thursday nights were spent at that park.

Tears, games and silence.

My case was still being investigated, but it became clear that punishment for Josh would be minimal. I continued to talk to more and more professionals. They even showed me pictures of female anatomy and asked me to point out each area where I was touched followed by and in depth explanation of how I was touched. I was alone in the room with a social worker. She drew a picture of female anatomy and was sitting across from me. I sat in a chair. This was in a small room at the Advocacy Center that I'd never been in.

For a third grader, this was some pretty heavy shit.

Later, I gave a victim impact statement to show how Josh's actions had affected my life. My father didn't come. I remember sitting in the courtroom, staring at Josh. He was wearing an orange jumpsuit with handcuffs keeping him in his seat. I stood at the stand and spoke into a small microphone that echoed my words around the courtroom.

Forcing myself to stay strong, but a steady stream of tears rolled down my cheeks for the majority of my speech. He sat emotionless the entire time. I don't understand what caused him to abuse me, and I never will. And those were the words I'd never forget saying.

"I'd never understand why he did it."

Josh got off easy. Simple probation. There wasn't much proof considering it was a *he said, she said* situation. The court kept my diary as evidence. I'd lost a friend; I'd lost my comfort.

All Josh had to do was refrain from excessive drinking, pass drug tests, and register as a sex offender. Josh already had a criminal record, a fact we found out later. He had been arrested for alcohol-related offences. Josh failed to register as a sex offender and was found drinking and driving. He ended up serving jail time and now lives in a city far away from me.

I was nine when the abuse happened and ten when I reported it. I am seventeen now.

This experience has changed me in so many ways, managing to come out so much stronger in the end. I never had the courage to stand up to my dad and all of the emotional abuse he put me through. Now, I haven't seen or talked to him in two years.

After my case was closed, our relationship only got worse. Therapists insisted that a relationship with my father was essential and crucial for my development. They continued to push a relationship that just wasn't going to happen. We continued to scream at each other at almost every visit. One day, it became too much and my father kicked me out and told me never to come back.

My mom picked me up, and I never continued visitation again. He tried to contact me a few times and even sent some happy birthday texts. Those stopped two years ago, my relationship with my mother is stronger than ever. I'm forever grateful for how hard she fought for justice during my case. She ignored everyone telling her that she was fighting a losing battle and never gave up. For that, I am forever thankful. Abuse is abuse. I am learning every day that every story matters, that I matter.

I matter.

Dear new diary. Dear bold line. I am inspired.

The Humble Servant

Servant: A person who performs duties for others, a devoted and helpful follower or supporter. Servant.

As a devoted servant, one of my many duties is that of an usher in church. Ushering in the church brings joy to my marrow, if joy were cells I'd be a human made up of cells of joy. A joy that would keep my body safe from harm, a joy that cures.

I get to welcome believers and non-believers. Passing by are old faces, new faces. A constant flow of people coming and people going like waves that hit the shore if only for a moment, making room for new waves, or waves that may have been hiding and suddenly rushing to the surface. Then there are waves that reach the shore and gently vanish, soaking into the sand. Those waves never come back.

The sound of the waves crashing loudly in my ears, squinting my eyes as the blinding sunlight hits my irises regulating the light, and I can return to a moment in my past and taste the salt of the ocean. I'm in the water with my brother, the happy little me splashing and sharing laughter.

As a young girl, there was no greater feeling than looking ahead with a secured sense of knowing. Knowing that someone was always there, that you are unconditionally loved.

Staring back at my mom and stepdad as they watched us enjoy every moment of the sun. With the heavens so blue, covering us. Sheltering us from all life's worries.

Sunday. I am the face they see early morning, with a smile so bright I'm certain it's my heart smiling because they feel it, I feel it. It's not just a smile; it's my heart. Handing out hugs so tight my gladness permeates into their lives. Let's not forget the kisses, every cheek different in texture and color, followed by a, "You look so beautiful today." The reality is, everyone is truly beautiful, but never always feels that way. But it is an inevitable truth, everyone in their imperfection of thoughts, or self-hate or for the lack of impersonating what beauty is to this selfish world. You are beautiful. A beautiful truth everyone deserves to experience, a truth everyone should accept.

A truth no man should ever be able to steal.

After connecting with so much beauty. I'll walk the individuals to their seats, making sure they have everything they need, or if they needed anything in particular, I'd assure them that I was there to serve and help. Directions to the bathroom, an extra chair, a Bible perhaps. Watching the hope and at times despair of the faces that enter this building, faces that express the war that was about to take place.

On a mission for an answer, a mission for healing, a mission of complete surrender. The mission begins, praying in desperation, crying out for an answer, believing with all their might. Praying that tomorrow will be a better day, waiting for that job, praying for a loved one, for that baby that life form in its early stages of growth to keep growing. For the son or daughter filling their veins with their addictions, for the husband that left, for the wife who is no longer interested in love.
Simply and absolutely alone with God.
Hands in the air as worship overtakes, the beating of the drums in sync with the heartfelt cries. A genuine cry for help whether it be for the person next to them or someone they've only met once. Nonetheless. A cry for the unknown.

A cry to that which is not seen. To the now empty cross.

To a Man who has risen from the dead.

The servant in me, always on her feet during the service, handing out envelopes for the offering, mothers hand their little children a few coins, the coins she never uses at the supermarket, coins she needs to get rid of or the only money she owns. She hands it over to add to the offering basket floating from one hand to another, building their fragile characters, preparing them to become givers of the purest form. An early understanding that giving physically does not always mean receiving.

An understanding of how many ways receiving shows itself.

Once we have all received our strength for the week, and the building once again becomes silent. It becomes an empty church with the echoes of worship slightly in the air. Accompanying the intense echoes of worship is the desperation and pain still lingering in certain parts of the atmosphere, some of the beautiful creatures managed to leave their hurt behind, yet in some places, the atmosphere is cleaner than it was before, it seems no one has breathed here.

As other beautiful humans decided to take their pain back home with them and lock it away until next Sunday. To hold the hands of their disappointment and pain secretly entertaining them.

To continually fill their jars of tears and gently store them away with the rest of the jars that are accumulating dust.

With every emotion in the atmosphere. Now, it's my duty to get everything back into its rightful place, together with my true friends, we'll clean the church up with zealous hearts. Every Bible handed out, put back. Every extra chair, stacked away with the rest. Every candy wrapping is picked up and thrown away, water bottles crushed. When a thought hits my skin, causing the hairs on my arms to stand erect.

I love it. I love what I do.

The words that are so bravely flowing might make me come across as the perfect human being, a woman who has it all together. Could being a servant truly cause this much satisfaction?

Picking up after people, showing them to the bathroom even though the sign clearly says *Toilet*. The servant that knows where she's going, the servant filled with hope. With a prison of hope for a heart, where discourage and hurt had no place in the blood pumping life to my heart to my existence.

My life was not always this moment; this present was not always my reality. Joy did not always fill my marrow; the cells of my body were once only pumping lies and corruption to my heart.

I was born in Haiti, but I came to the United States of America when I was only six years old, I then went back to Haiti when I was about eleven years old. I may be in the land where dreams come true, but I miss my country very much. Where I may not have had as much as much as I do now, where happiness filled everything that lacked.

The feeling of belonging kept me alive.

☐I was a sweet and sometimes loving child. What child isn't difficult at some stage in life, or stubborn? It's all part of being a child, a part of growing.

An excuse to throw tantrums and cry until I'd eventually get my way, and other times just had to stop crying because what I wanted was never going to happen. Then, the smiles would return. And the love stronger. Love that would never forsake me, no matter my phase in life.

Like every young girl, I thoroughly loved to play outside with my family and friends. It filled me with an overwhelming amount of emotions, so overwhelmed it was released in the form of smiles and giggling. Every now and then I'd just stare and enjoy their faces. Sometimes my family would watch us play, laughing and mumbling amongst themselves. Grown up things I guess. No matter their conversation or private jokes, no matter the game, laughter was the food that filled every soul, especially when playing games with my friends.

I was surrounded by my entire world in one place.

The fun never stopped, we were children, innocent and full of imagination just waiting to explode. Arguments were few simply because they didn't last long enough to ruin the imagination we needed to fulfil.

Then there were times where I'd play with my baby dolls like every little girl does.

Alone in the in a room, or in a corner. The dolls so real, everyone else walking around didn't exist. My ears blocked out every voice. Mommy's voice calling out that it was time for dinner almost frustrated me. It annoyed me because I only wanted to give my dolls every minute of my attention.

One baby doll in particular was white with blue eyes. At times if I'd shake her hard enough were able to blink, even though she could blink now and then she was stubborn and still without expression and if I stared at her ice blue eyes long enough the depth and stillness. It almost scared me; my baby doll was still the company I preferred. We had nothing in common but I enjoyed her company, she was the lead role in every game my imagination invented at that moment. The blue-eyed doll was everything to me, some days she was a mother, other days a friend, perhaps even a nurse. She was so versatile in her role play she could even become my baby. I suppose this was the love I had for her. She could be anything I needed her to be. Oddly enough, as much as we were friends, she had no name. None of them had names.

The baby dolls kindly changing their role in my imagination, blinking on demand, allowing me to pull on their hair and I hadn't named any of them.

How could they belong without a name?

Being a child was bliss until unwanted shadows started to appear. Even happiness has a shadow. Shadows are colorless, they are black, faceless and they hold no expression, but with careful, intricate detail, they'll follow you eternally. One of my shadows revealed itself in the form of my grandfather. An unpleasant shadow with a life of its own. My prison of hope fighting to keep the hurt from seeping into my heart.

We lived in a small two-bedroom apartment in New York City. A home that brought happiness and where we were stable capable of laughing. Where mom would always talk to us about God. I knew who He was, whether I grasped the concept of someone, One man dying for the sins of the entire world was not an easy thing to digest. I listened, either way, the stories fascinated me and almost comforted me. How was I suppose to accept this kind of forgiveness my mother was talking about?

Did I need forgiveness at such a young age?

Until I discovered happiness that had many shadows. A dark side of happiness. The superficial side. Strange things started taking place in the minute living room next to my grandfather's bedroom. The beginning of an evil shadow that would never leave me. He loved staring at me, his eyes uncomfortably on me. The first encounter with a confusion that caused me to become mute, his hands on my young body. It wasn't right, and I knew it. There was nothing I could say.

I'd silently freeze and die at the same time. There was no possible way my heart was beating while his hands fondled my breasts. He was my grandfather; he was a shadow. Fear had a hold on my nine-year-old self, clenching its nails into my skin, bruising me until the bruises became wounds. Deep wounds.

I started wetting the bed. My gut says my mother knew something was going on behind closed door no, in front of her very eyes. That wouldn't stop her from forcing me to give him a hug when I'd get home from school. *Hate*, a word so powerful it damages and corrupts the state of mind and the heart's ability to beat normally.

Instead of a beating heart once filled with warm blood, my blood was frozen, and I hated having to wrap my arms around him, having his body that close to mine. I was the snow, and he was the dirty footsteps ruining the image of purity and innocence.

Afraid of this man of this most annoying breath of a shadow. Mother must have known, the help in her voice and action evident as it reaches out. It reached out without saying a word.

A quiet comfort for a loud hurt.

That's when real forms of shadows started appearing before my eyes. Shadows who had faces and were in color, they appeared so real I'd urge to touch them, even though I really couldn't. Unafraid at their welcoming appearance. Bobby who was a fat and chubby little boy. And then there's Sue who was thin and very pretty with blonde long hair and Sandy who was also thin with long golden hair they were the ones who always played with me always encouraged me whenever I was scared and or nervous I could always count on them to be there. They made everything easier, every game became more fun and going to bed became easier as they would comfort every fear.

Were they the best thing that happened to my life at the time?

No, because there were two things they couldn't do, that was stopping me from pulling out my hair. Hair that I'd pluck out of my skull until the age of 30. The plucking escalated. My nerves now sending messages to my brain, kindly helping me, talking to my hands and to my mouth to open up wide. I'd put the hair in my mouth. I'd eat it.

The second thing they were unable to help with was the molestation that had taken place. They were too late! They were not real! And there was no way on earth they were able to stop what would then take place.

Pieces of the darkest shadows, like flashes of streetlights hitting my closed eyelids.

As life would have it, I turned thirteen that's when my friends and boyfriends got me into drugs and alcohol. There was now no turning back, the effect wasn't long lasting, but the need to stay in that state of numbness was the addiction. Where my body could feel and the blood pumping through me was finally warm.

The state of knowing everything was really nothing.

Fear and hurt. You are nothing.

Then, reality struck. The numbness, addiction and I, we were waves crashing into rocks. Because I then was left with nothing. I became the mist of the wave. I had no family, and no friends to turn to for help. So, I ended up homeless on the street and would start selling my body for food, drugs and alcohol.

I was now at the age of fourteen when I desperately attempted to kill myself. The pills weren't strong enough. Even though I had ice running through my veins, my loneliness and the ice-cold blood mixed with pills wasn't enough to kill me. Then life welcomed me to a home; the home was a mask. The mask was a mental institution. I remember the hospital, it was like a home with many different children. Every child had had enough of life in here it seems. They placed me in a room that was all white. White like the pure snow I once was. Until the shadows pursued me. The beds were small, and everyone had their own beds, the sheets were white, the rooms were small but cold.

Every window in every room had bars, so there was no escaping at all. I was in a room with two or three other girls. We'd have to attend meetings where we would have to talk about our problems.

Frustrated. My heart was frustrated. Because: I WAS NOT THE PROBLEM! THE HANDS OF THAT SHADOW, THE COMFORT OF THAT DRUG, BOBBY, SUE AND SANDY. YOU LEFT! YOU ARE THE PROBLEM!

Getting older didn't help either, life still wanted me alive to suffer. All that was left was to bow down as its humble servant. Life was laughing at me. Her laughter had to stop, so I tried again to killed myself. The small, potent pink pills stared at me just lying in the palm of my hand. Internally, secretly I begged them to work. To stop my aching heart, to do what Bobby, Sandy and Sue couldn't do. Do the thing everyone including me has failed to do. Take my life. Take it like every shadow does, ruthless and merciless in their taking.

I give you the permission.

☐I was fifteen years old the first time I sold my body. The humble servant still out, roaming the streets, owned. Owned by my best friend's uncle, he was my pimp. I belonged to another human. I belonged to the flesh. The men I'd encounter were usually older men. Men who'd use me and go back to their lives far from me, I was a few minutes of disturbing pleasure in their lives.

Like my baby doll with blue eyes and curly hair, who never had any expression. No expression, especially when I so much needed her to say something or to wink at me. We now finally had something in common. I'd stare into nothing, while these shadows took everything from me, everything that was not theirs to have. I became the baby doll. She was now playing with me.

The truth is, I no longer knew what was mine. There was no emotion while selling my body.

Was this giving?

Eventually, it depended on the men if they were very old sometimes I would feel filthy because of their age but, I eventually got over it. When I finally made money, I would buy myself some alcohol, drugs, and food maybe pizza or potato chips.

Something I managed to own for a moment.

Another flash in front of my closed eyelids, this time it was not the streetlights, no it's the shadows running circles around me, sucking harshly on my soul for whatever life might be left. Life wouldn't take me, and here I was giving involuntarily, numb, owned and kidnapped. I was held at gunpoint for three days and three nights. The gun was cold reminding me of the metal bars in the institution.

Immorally raped by eight different young boys and men.

I was extremely scared. They were possessed with an imitation of power, but I saw it. That hint of distraction, a sense of guilt was the hint of distraction. Not all of them had it, but some of them did. Subconsciously with desperation trying to make that guilt disappear, they'd talk louder. The more the power possessed them, the more they convinced their hearts that it wasn't guilt. It was sheer power.

I wasn't as numb as I'd thought all along because I didn't yet feel like death was an option at this moment. I knew it wasn't an option because I feared it. I feared death. This fear made me conscious, helped the little life left in me find its rhythm.

Life, are you still dwelling in me?

I thought I was definitely going to die. No doubt this time. The time I feared, is the time it had to happen. It was the way of the world; you want what you can't have, you have what you never asked for. Echoes of that laughter that filled my early years as a child, times where I had no care in the world. That security of staring back at my mom and stepdad on that bright sunny day. Or staring at the world, I was surrounded by for a split second. Taking it all in. Their faces vague, they become mist.

Everything was nothing.

After three long days. They told me they would kill me if I ever reported it. There was still air in my lungs. My body sore and my eyes open.

Life, are you still dwelling in me?

The self-realization that I had fallen a slave to my crisis was when I was in my late twenties. Still homeless, even my heart was homeless. Still, on the street selling my body, I knew at that point my life was definitely over.

An odd knowing that I didn't physically need to be buried in the ground to be dead. A strange magic power you have due to pain, an eccentric, painful and magical phenomenon.

Dead and alive at the same time. Life's worst trick.

Where most people are concerned with what they are going to do next month, or where they would vacation in the Summer in the midst of a cold winter. I had to think about what I was going to do every minute and every hour of my day. Sometimes I would sleep over at a friend's house while their parents were at work or I would sleep in the park outside of apartments. A good night's rest was my imagination, was in the short bursts of dreams I'd have.

Other than the imaginations and dreams I would have to walk around until morning time. The nights dark and hot outside I felt dirty and filthy so unclean. People never paid any attention to me everyone would mind their own business.

My baby doll still playing games with her imagination. Just as I'd stop the world around me to play with her, she stopped the world from ever seeing me.

They were blind.

I wasn't there. Everything was nothing.

There will never be such a thing as the right words; the right words don't exist. All I was, was unhappy, unworthy and just depressed. This was the lowest of the lowest. The only lowest that I was yet to experience was physical death. The only echoes now ringing in my ears are the words of my shadows assuring me that I would never amount to anything.

"You're ugly, and you will never amount to anything."

...

One of my classmates in school that I was attending at the time had invited me to visit her church. Open to new ideas and new ways, besides, I always knew who Jesus was thanks to mothers stories.

I went to church with my friend, apprehensive and with my heart guarded. Standing there was a man so certain of the words coming out of his mouth and he the Pastor started preaching. We might as well have been just the two of us in the room alone; every word was made for me, it was so powerful and beautiful I started crying hysterically that's when the opportunity had arisen that if we were ready, we could come up for prayer and receive Jesus. Something called the inside of my heart, without thinking twice I got up, went to the altar and decided I was tired of living the life I was living. I was so tired. That day, February 12, 2013, I gave my life to Jesus Christ. Uncertain of what was to follow, but I knew I was doing the right thing.

The days that followed I spent seeking a personal relationship with God. I started praying and reading the Bible. And getting involved in the church doing different activities and being around positive people, these were all things that made the transition easy.

Listening to others share their testimonies, filling myself with only the positive. Learning to love again and being compassionate from a once ice cold heart. Then came my time to be someone else's help, for them to use my pain for their healing. There is always a sense of healing when you know you're not alone, in knowing someone can understand. The first time I spoke about my traumatic experience was when I attended this support group at my church called *Celebrate Recovery.* Embarrassed perhaps ashamed but it was therapeutic. I finally understood and accepted the love and forgiveness I received from Jesus Christ.

...

I am now in school studying for my High school diploma I'm also an usher and with great joy greet everyone at my church. Every Wednesday morning me and my fellow church members go to the nursing homes to Preach and volunteer we also visit hospitals and pray for people and show them the love of Jesus Christ, not always in the form of words, but by the example of our character.

I'm also part of a group where I help and counsel young women who are victims of domestic and sexual abuse. I truly believe that God allowed me to go through what I went through to be able to help others.

This may be a difficult concept to grasp, but it is my truth. And all I ask is for you to accept it without judgement. I believe we have enough of that going around.

There are so many people out there that are crying out for help we have to be bold enough to speak out against violence.

Life has also finally had mercy on me, for I am also a happy mother of four beautiful and healthy children, my life experience has helped me to become a more loving, caring and more understanding mother towards my children. My sense of protection regarding my children grows stronger with every moment of their growing pains and joys. I'm very careful of whom I have around my kids I don't trust just anyone and everyone around my children.

So much of myself I get to see in my children. The way I used to love to play patty-cake when I was little my youngest daughter loves to play the same game. At it brings her the same joy and feeling that she is surrounded by her world.

Also, just as I used to have three different imaginary friends my son used to have an imaginary friend that he played with but thank God, he grew out of that (giggling). My baby doll who was my quiet company accompanied my children as well in their younger stages.

When I look at my kids, losing myself in their beauty, I see their innocence, innocence I once had. Don't get me wrong they are children; they sometimes tell lies like most children because they don't want to get into trouble, in all honesty, I used to lie about everything when I was little especially when it came down to stealing, which I was regrettably good at. That's why I teach my kids to always be honest with me no matter what.

With the years passing and their trust in me as a mother always maturing, I thank God that my kids can come and talk to me about anything and everything. That is something that I wasn't able to do with my mother while growing up till now, but I'm realizing there is no such thing as a perfect mom we all make mistakes we are all human. As much we love our kids, we are also capable of suffocating them, finding that balance will only come with time. Without a doubt I'll get there, so will you.

I am now learning to take each day one day at a time asking God to help me to be a better mom towards my kids each and every day.

...

To myself in the future:

I hope five years from now you'll have your own business.
You will be going back to your country soon. It is God's will that you help the children up there, it is part of your calling and dreams to be a missionary. You're going to travel the world to help the children of the world. And you are going to be great at it. Remember always to look back into your life and see what God has brought you out of. Remind yourself and others that all things are possible with the help of God. To myself in the future remember continually be very grateful for everything not everything is for nothing. You learned a lot from your experience and mistakes of course, but everything you went through, every experience was to build your character, to mould and shape you into this great and wonderful woman that you are now.

To anyone who has hurt me in the past, to the hate you have shown towards me, to the abuse and for stealing most of my life, give me this moment to let you know. I truly forgive you.

Simply put, because forgiveness is not saying that what you did was okay, that the pain you caused will be a distant memory. It doesn't even mean that you have gotten away with what you have done. No. I forgive you for my freedom, for my healing to take place and for my deliverance over the shadows you have constantly placed in my life. I forgive you to say; you have no more power over me, I forgive you for you to be free and to be healed.

I truly forgive you. I forgive you for my wellbeing.

To the media, I think it's very disturbing and disgusting the way the media view women. A lot of the music videos make it seem as if women only have one purpose and that's that women are objects of sex, objects used to fulfil the one minded desires. They show no respect towards women, it makes me sick especially as a mother of three young daughters. Even women towards women, we are to be inspiring one another, not breaking each other down.

Women are more than sex objects we are mothers, daughters, career women, housewives. We are smart, beautiful and strong. Beauty must be more than just showing your skin.

Get your message straight, for your children and the generation after us.

To the government, it is unfortunate how survivors do more for victims than you do. We are failing in creating awareness on educating the world on all forms of sexual abuse. Even the poor pick one another up. How rape survivors can only heal when one speaks up. There must be more you can do...

The experience that I went through as a child and as an adult has made me stronger and wiser. I now know that everything I went through in my life was to get me prepared for the obstacles that I would be facing throughout my journey. I'm also able to help others who have been through the same experience that I went through, Christian or not. True love and compassion and the willing to listen is a profound form of extending help.

I'm a more loving, caring and forgiving person and I know if I can make it this far then with the help of Jesus Christ I'm able to succeed anywhere.

God is Love that's the first and most important of all lessons I have learnt. I am now able to give and receive love because of What Jesus Christ did for me when He died on the cross so I could be free. You also have to love yourself, you have to be able to forgive those who hurt you. It will not be something that will happen overnight it takes years it is a process, everything in life is a process. For me, the ability to receive healing and the only way through all of that was to ask Jesus Christ into my heart. He's the only one that can heal and deliver every past and future pain that you will ever have or had experienced. Love to me is forgiveness, caring, patience, self-control, compassion. Love is a word of action, love is saying that you are sorry when you hurt someone whom you love and turning away from doing wrong but truly living a life that truly pleases God. However, no matter your religion, your choice of healing. With all the fake freedom we are surrounded with, know that forgiveness is vital. Forgive to save yourself from falling deeper into the darkness of the world.

Be brave.

Fearfully Young

Angel: Hey there's a party tonight. You want to go?

Me: Yeah sure. Whose house is it at?

Angel: It's at James' house.

Me: Oh I don't know him that well. You sure I can come?

Angel: Yeah it's fine. In his eyes, the more girls there are, the better.

Me: Ok. I'll get dressed and meet you at your house.

Angel: Great!

This call was nothing out of the norm, especially when you are referred to as the "Party Starter." Getting invited to parties where I hardly knew the people, at times I didn't know them at all, was completely normal. The endless beauty of being young and free. That's how it works, you know a friend, a friend calls a friend that's having a party, they end up calling you, and that's it. A night out.

Before the call, I had immersed my focus into my YouTube channel. Planning out new videos and responding to e-mails.

The new world also known as the internet can be a pleasant place for independent artists, a place to set your creativity free.

The battle for attention intense at times. Blogging, vlogging, make-up tutorials you name it, someone out there does it. Not certain on how to use life's basics? The internet will tell you. One of the many pressures accompanied with being on social media is how many likes and subscriptions you are receiving. Sharing your life helps your status. Part of social media is sharing most of your life, and here I was sitting, remembering that call. How it changed my life, uncertain if I should press record and say it out loud. As much as there are encouraging people walking the earth, in the new world (internet) people can be vicious, ruthless and can easily ridicule you from the comfort of their homes. Without ever meeting you or physically harm you. Words that are used for the innermost expression of love, used for all things beautiful, are now in this new world indifferent to weapons. Words have become weapons of destruction.

I'll do it, I'll tell my story. I'll make this video and tell the new world my story.

Record.

Staring at myself in the camera, fixing my hair nervously fidgeting. My fingers through my thick curly hair, suddenly my mind goes blank. And I don't know where to begin. I'll make a joke! Perfect idea, jokes and laughter are my masks. Awkward silence makes me uncomfortable. A joke could not hold back my tears, the joke assisted my tears to my ducts, causing my eyes to become glossy. Ruining my make-up was not an option. Every time I'd manage to calm myself down the tears crept back. Tilting my head back, forcing the tears to leave my eyes. Grunting, sighing feeling overwhelmingly annoyed with myself. Keep it together. My eyes back on the camera. And my mind fast forwards back to the call that would change everything.

Angel: Hey there's a party tonight. You want to go?

Me: Yeah sure. Whose house is it at?

Angel: It's at James' house.

Me: Oh I don't really know him that well. You sure I can come?

Angel: Yeah it's fine. In his eyes, the more girls there are, the better.

Me: Ok. I'll get dressed and meet you at your house.
Angel: Great!

Getting ready, psyching myself up for a party wasn't hard. All I needed was to listen to my African music, some Caribbean and my twerking music. It always gets me in the mood to party. I lived in Maryland for ten years. My family is from Africa, Kenya to be exact. My parents currently live in Kenya and come from a fairly large family. I have six siblings. Three are older than me, and three are younger. Three of them are in the states. Two are in Sweden, and one is in Kenya with my dad.

With that said, music fixed a lot.

The decision process of what to wear wasn't hard at all; I went to the party super casual. I did a light layer of make-up; I wore some jeans and a sweater. Young, free and I even had the luxury of having my own car. What more could a girl ask for? I drove to Angel's house, and she drove. I was expecting to drink, so I didn't want to drive.

Upon our arrival, it was clear the party that we ended up at wasn't a party. Yes, there was alcohol and some people, but it wasn't a party unless there was dancing. People were sitting throwing back shots of liquor with haste. Some were smoking weed. There was music playing but very quietly. Scanning the area, I noticed that there were a few people I knew from high school scattered around the room and also some girls I knew.

Being the type of person that never suffered from the sense of not belonging, I adapted to every situation and every kind of person, confident in myself I went straight to the girls I knew amongst the familiar faces was my best friend, Bella. Bella is three years younger than me. She's also African. We met through Angel's little sister.

Bella: Hey girl! How've you been?

Me: Pretty good. Just been working and not much else

Bella: That's cool. I'm still trying to find a job.

Me: You should apply where I work.

Bella: I'll definitely do that. I'll text you later this week for the details.

Me: Ok

The party was pretty dull; I walked over to the coffee table where the drinks sat, and I decided to have a drink. I trusted myself with alcohol, I know my limits also I take pride in being the confident, independent 22-year old I was at this time.

One thing you should know about me is that I'm the definition of a heavyweight.

I have to take about ten shots just to feel tipsy. Keep that in mind.

I decided to take a shot of the only clear alcohol they had which was *Smirnoff* vodka. I've had *Smirnoff* many times before. It's not my favorite, but I wasn't going to drink any of the dark liquor they had. The *Smirnoff* hardly touched, as most people were into the *Hennessey*. Either way, I took a shot of the clear liquor. I didn't feel anything after, feeling that I could indeed handle another, during the evening I had two more.

That's when I felt it; it wasn't me. I am capable of drinking; my body started feeling heavy and my eyes back on the party. Paying close attention to the music playing vaguely in the background was rap and hip hop. Everybody was dressed casually. Mainly jeans. Chilled and enjoying the atmosphere. After being at the party for a while, the entire place smelled like weed.

Ignoring the heavy sensation, I went on to talk to the people I knew from high school. We spoke for a bit until I started to feel lightheaded. I told my friend Angel or *party buddy*.

We used to be close and at one time were best friends, but grew apart. And at parties were fairly close. Finally, I had to admit I was not feeling well. Something didn't add up, once the assurance hit me that I wasn't feeling too well.

She talked to the host of the party, and he said that I could lie down in his bedroom.
She thanked him and put me on his bed.

I remember the bed being pretty big; it must have been a queen-sized bed at least. The bed had a gold headboard all the walls were white. It was a master bedroom, so It had a bathroom in the bedroom. My body on the unknown sheets, my head spinning a slight breeze of anxiety floats over me. I didn't understand what was wrong with me. I've never felt anything after three shots.
Maybe there was something in it? But there's no way. I've known these guys since high school. I didn't know the owner of the house, but if he had put something in the drink, then my friends would have said something to me. Right?

Clearly, I am losing my mind; I trust all of them.

This is not the first party, I had partied with them before, and nothing was ever put in my drink. We partied together at least two weekends in a month. Perhaps more at times. I didn't even know what it felt like to be drugged.
My memory foggy, it must have been the state I was in as I don't know how much later after I was placed on the enormous bed when I heard the door open. Unable to open my eyes, they feel so heavy as if two anchors were holding them down and I was fighting with it.

Forcing them to open a little bit and I see Angel and James, James was the host of the party. They came and sat next to the bed. The buzzing of their whispers was all I could hear, every so often as they whispered they'd look over at me. No staring occurred, just whispers and the I guess *caring* look that fell on me every so often. I must have surprised them too by being as out of my mind as I was with three shots.

Confused about everything, the anchors have officially weighed my eyes down causing me to fall asleep.

Don't cry. Don't cry.

Tilting my tears back into its place, my eyes meet the camera once more, and I go back to telling the world my story.

Then all of a sudden James starts touching me. That's when I realize somebody else is in the room; we were not alone. It was Louis. Louis is one of my friends from high school. Louis was skinny, with a shaved head, very confident if not over confident.

I've known him for at least eight years. Knew his family and I would always greet him and his brothers. We were all friends. Even his father knew me as I would greet and even have a conversation with his dad on occasion. He was friends with my cousin Mark. Did I need more confirmation?

Yes, I know Louis, but I'm wondering why he's not saying anything to James. Why is Angel not saying anything to James? Does she, no maybe she thinks that this is what I want?

That I want to sleep with Louis. She wasn't a good enough judge as my friend if that's what she thought. I tell him to stop and Angel giggles, a giggle that echoed in my drowning ears. Somehow, I ended up on the floor with them, and James keeps trying to kiss me. James, the host I knew nothing of. My guess was they wanted to have a foursome. I'm not one to sleep around at all. James and Angel end up going to the bathroom and left me with Louis. What happened between Angel and James; no one will ever know. All I knew at that point was this; I was in a situation I didn't know how to get out of.

Louis starts touching me. I tell him to stop, and he just says relax. I start fading in and out of consciousness, anchored eyes, drowning ears and a heavy, slow voice. Why is he doing this? I thought we were friends and I could trust him.

I keep fading in and out. Every moment I was conscious, stop was the only word that came out of my mouth.

I'm conscious. I tell him to stop and get off of me, but I can't move my hands to where I want them to go. I want to push him off but I can't. I don't understand. What is wrong with me?

My hands weighty, my strength drained into the ground. Tied down fighting gravity. Louis was the gravity, the gravity that tied me down and took advantage of me. Uncertain of whether being unable to remember much could be an advantage because the hurt that followed was unbearable. The confusion, the questions far too overcoming.

I wake up the next morning feeling as if though a huge mountain had fallen on me, recklessly and intentionally. Picking myself up, my aim was to go home. No, I didn't say anything to anybody, not a word. Feeling stupid for drinking liquor that was not mine, feeling like it was all my fault, but also knowing that I had been taken advantage of. Left me with a sense of uncleanliness, confusion cheered me on the entire time, fear and shame all consumed me.

I didn't know what to think about what had happened. I needed to talk to somebody, but I didn't know how. I was scared people would think I was a slut, afraid that the story would be turned inside out and become the story where I got wasted and had sex with someone I never wanted to sleep with in the first place. Nobody would know that there was more to my story, how I suddenly lost my ability to think straight after drinking the alcohol no one else was touching. Feeling awkward in my silence, I rode to angel's house with her and Bella.

I didn't go home that morning; we ended up going to their place, I slept over and went home before she woke up.

Mixed feelings, who do I hate most right now?

Angel. Louis or myself?

Instead of heading home, I then decided to go and visit some of my other friends who live about an hour away from me. A part of me searching for a comfort, searching for understanding and the answer to all of this madness I couldn't touch, so far out of my reach, for my mind was not within me. When I get there, we decide to get some food. On the drive there, we started to have some girl talk. We were going to Fridays. Olga was driving, and Emily was sitting in the passenger seat. They are also African. Olga is Emily's older sister. I met them through Angel, and we became very close. Olga is like an older sister to me. When I need advice, I will always go to her, maybe the reason I never went home and headed over to see her. Emily is a little party animal, vivacious she was a runner in high school, and she was twenty at the time of this most unfortunate and confusing event.

Girl talk commenced, even though no talking would have been just fine with me, simply because any girl knows when girl talk takes place, it's detailed. Nothing is left out.

You're a chicken when you leave out details. Or you choose not to be too specific, and they'll take the answer as a *yes*. What you wanted the response to be was up to you. Chicken? It happened. Or it didn't. Humans are confusing this way.

"So how many people have you had sex with?" Close friends, they have this sixth sense about everything!

"Well after the other night, three."

"What do you mean? I want details!" Details I did not possess, details I too was searching for in the fog of my so-called brain.

"Yeah. Are you keeping secrets from us?" Emily joined in on Olga's curiosity rant.

There you go, the opportunity. Chicken? Did it happen? Or didn't it?

"No. So, this is what happened. I went to a party at James house, that Angel invited me to. They had liquor there, and I drank some. From that point, I don't remember what happened. I kept blacking out. Louis had sex with me. I didn't want to, though. I remember telling him to get off, but he didn't so it happened."
I responded the way a 2-year-old walks. Slow, inconsistent. Stuttering and indecisive.

"Girl, That's rape."

"What do you mean?"

"You told him, *no,* and you were wasted. You couldn't consent, so it's rape. It sounds like you could have been drugged too."

"What the fuck?" Who do I listen to at this point? The fear which is vivid in my eyes in the form of a gun pointed at my head the steel sealed to my skin, or my friend, my best friend. I've been betrayed by a friend a couple of hours ago, what and who could I trust? Her words in my head. *You've been drugged. You've been raped. I've been raped.*

"Are you ok?" Sympathy hits Olgas voice.

"Yeah I'm fine." I wasn't fine. I can't believe I didn't realize what this was. I never thought it would happen to me. What do I do now? Do I confront him? Do I call the cops? How could somebody I've known for years do this to me? How can I call the cops on him? Our families know each other. We go to the same church. I'm a friend to his brothers. What do I do?

This changes everything, my world as I knew it changed, shaken like a Christmas snow globe.

The snowflakes scattered as they fall, were the pieces of my life that now no longer make any sense.

Shaking the snow globe harder. The few things I could remember played back in my head, all the time. I would remember saying *no*. Him on top of me. Hearing Angel in the bathroom. Her giggle echoing. Shake the snow globe harder! Flashes of me not being able to push him off of me. Every flash, repeating itself. Then, I allowed the snowflakes to settle.

Sleeping, something so normal and well needed became a pain. The very thought of having to go to bed caused an indescribable anxiety. I would wake up shaking in the middle of the night. It got better, but I still get nightmares. The new world... was I going to share this?

I'm blank for a moment, still recording but blank.

As hard as it may be to believe. I never told the cops about what happened to me. I never confronted Louis about it either. I've seen Louis around a couple of times, and every time I'm near him I freeze up. The first time I saw him, I had a panic attack.

The reality of what had happened to me far too real. The disappointment I felt towards myself all came rushing back into my head. I couldn't say anything; the snow globe is shaken viciously every time I'd see him. I just panicked.

I saw him twice at two different parties. He didn't act differently towards me, his life, his snow globe remained untouched. Remained, everything it wasn't it remained something that looked normal to the person looking in. We didn't speak at all, though. Usually, I'm the one to start conversations with everybody. But no conversation was going to happen here. I knew my truth, and it was unfathomable.

Since I didn't call the cops on him, Olga thinks I need to at least confront him. The reason for not going to the cops was simple.
I didn't want to go to the cops and have them not believe me. Because everyone's mind was within them, besides mine, who involuntarily was silenced by whatever was lurking in the poison I had trusted to drink. This was the biggest mistake of my life. If I had said something, I would have been able to sleep better because I would know he couldn't do this to any other girl. That is my biggest regret.

People tell me that I need to get through this and get over it. *Get over it,* like it's a knee-high box standing in my way. When I hear the words "get over it" I sink internally, the words in my head indirectly meant that they doubt what happened. They don't believe me. It's like they don't realize that I'm trying, they don't know that it's not something you shove into your closet, it's quite the opposite.

It's that annoying item of clothing that keeps falling out no matter how many times you attempt to shove it back in. My closet needed fixing, that would mean taking out every item of clothing, folding it neatly, then placing it back in creating space for everything. So I can choose items with confidence. I don't want to be scared anymore. Every time I see a man pass me on the street, I think they're going to attack me. I know it doesn't make sense, but that's just how I feel. I can't explain it.

Before this happened, I didn't even know what a panic attack was. Now I get them weekly, and I don't want to talk to my friends about it. I just don't ever bring it up and they don't ask about it. I think it made them uncomfortable to talk about it. That gun pointing at my head. Fear. Tells me they'll probably just think I'm being dramatic and wanting attention. I don't talk to anybody, and that's not right.

Talking to the new world about this. The internet. My camera still faithfully recording. Yes, it has made me realize that I can't run away from this. It's affecting my everyday life, and I need to work on getting better. That there was no joke I could conjure up; no witty response would be able to cover up this awkwardness.
For the first time, I am having to deal with being uncomfortable, because it is serious. I have a long way to go.

The miles of my healing almost seem endless. After writing this, I'm going to look up some therapists and support groups. I can't be afraid of getting help because I need it. I can't let what happened to me change the way I live my everyday life. Oh. I smile at the camera for a moment. I can't be afraid of getting help because I need it. I can't let what happened to me change the way I live my everyday life. These words. I find something positive about it; It can't possibly... it's possible. This makes me a survivor. Naked truth. Meet bravery.

To anybody reading this, please know that you're not alone. There are people you can talk to. If you're scared to report the person that attacked you, just know you can do it. Be strong. I don't want anybody else to feel the regret I feel every day for not reporting my attacker. To experience the whirlwind of emotions gnawing away at your flesh on a daily basis.

My healing must start somewhere, but for now, I hold no forgiveness in my heart. Either I'll have to confront Louis, watching him walking around as if nothing happened allows that gun pointing at my head to fire shots.
I hadn't spoken about the attack out loud after talking to Olga. So, here you go the world.
I sat down to talk about it on video; I broke down, I am broken, my shaken walls have fallen.

All my feelings came up, and it was very hard to get through. I'm scared to post it. I hadn't told anybody in my family what had happened to me, so I know they are going to be calling me asking what happened. And wondering why I didn't tell them or go to the police. Questions that I didn't know how to answer. I may not have the answers just yet. This is my beginning.

I'll start and finish as a survivor, not as the girl who had been raped.

...

Louis. What you did was disgusting, no sign of human behaviour in what you did. I live every day in fear because of what you did. A guy smiles at me, and I get scared. When I go to a bar, I can never let anybody buy me a drink. I spend my nights constantly waking up at night terrified, reliving the attack. While you sleep peacefully. Your dreams contain every shade of the colour spectrum. Whereas mine is black. I would have never even kissed you if I were in my right mind. What you did disfigured me for life. But know that in my heart of hearts, I will not let you win. You will not have this power over me. I wish every day that I wouldn't have gone to that party. I wish I never would have met you.

Love
Everywhere

As I slowly close my eyes to the sunlight, I invite inside a darker world. Acceptance for my circumstance is not about being okay with what happened; it's about becoming okay with not being okay. It's not about forcing anything. It's sitting with the pain, feeling it from every cell in my body and not running away from these harrowing feelings. To have enough courage to collapse into nothingness and to recognize the body that is still standing here.

Strong and brave.

I open my eyes; the sunlight is beaming into my pores like liquid gold. Although I've daydreamed of dying, I usually don't feel suicidal. Death doesn't look like anything. Death feels like nothingness, dissolving into an infinite vast pool of the darkest oxygen. Releasing the borders of this physical body and releasing this perspective similarly to us as we lay to rest every night, slowly drifting off into another dimension.

Sometimes, a few days go by without me becoming triggered by the wounds of my past. These wounds ripple outward into my present moment. I am still learning how it feels to live safely and securely.

Time is the true healer of all wounds. Within these wounds, new flowers spring from the dusty pavements of my past. These flowers teach me lessons of compassion and empathy for all life. My outer skin smiled while my inner being was reading a story dripping with disorientation. I was falling apart, slowly being ripped by my seams and unraveled piece by piece, my deconstruction - my old ways of thinking were no longer serving me. Like the process of a caterpillar becoming a butterfly, I had to completely break down every part of who I thought I was, and become something new. Something unknown.

Once I found this new light, like dewy air on a sweet morning after a long dark winter, this new way of living that allowed me to free my mind and enjoy life with an open heart- not just pretend to be happy, but to feel true joy and connection with myself and others.

I was molested repetitively for two monstrous years. These two years of my budding life were the most difficult to bear on every front. Mentally, physically, and emotionally.

I believed, down to the center of my core, that I was to blame for what happened to me, and that it was completely my fault and I only got what I was asking for.

I was a girl, falling into the painful depths of self-hatred and self-mutilation. I was hurting myself for so many reasons, perhaps for every reason, I could find under the sun. As I would slowly slice my flesh, I would feel the pain that everyone had shushed away from me. The pain that I was never allowed to feel, and even better... now I had control over it. I would allow it to come when I pleased and was able to control the depth of the cut. I imagined the more I bled, the more my sorrows were washed away. I was a depressed adolescent.

It's the summer before high school, like any young girl, I thought I understood everything. I got a job through a family friend and was excited to finally earn some of my own money. I could use it for whatever I wanted, and I felt a sense of responsibility. I was welcomed to this Italian bakery by the aromas of delicious bread in the morning, and throughout the day, cakes pastries and gelato... mounds of cookies, more cookies than anyone could ever eat.

My favorite were the mini St. Joseph's pastries, an ornate doughnut filled with cannoli creme or custard decorated with more creme, toasted coconut and a cherry.

My days were soon spent inside these bakery walls. There were many people working in the back; they started their day before the sun rose and left work in the afternoon. There were a few girls working at the counter; we would all gossip about the people in our lives and complain about our evil manager. Her presence intimidated me. The owner of this bakery always looked at me with big eyes. Young and sure of myself. I knew it all. The truth was, I knew nothing.

He was an Italian man in his late sixties. He would talk to me so sweetly and gently. I was his princess. He treated me special from all the other girls and even more special than I felt from anyone else in my life. He always told me how much he loved me, how he cared for me. After a few months, he started adding extra money in my weekly paycheck, sometimes hundreds of dollars. I wondered if he did the same for the other girls, but I knew better than to ask questions if I wanted that to continue.

I would feel pangs of jealousy at times when he would flirt with other girls, then feel guilty and ashamed for this resentment. He had a wife, and a son who could be my father... we all believed they were part of the mafia; different men would be walking in and out suspiciously, they convene in groups and have 'meetings' in the back. I am anxious and paranoid, but once I swear I heard him speaking in his office about a body. When he yelled, everyone felt the anger and fear.

Our relationship grew slowly; he gradually pushed my boundaries to see how far he could go. The first time he kissed me on the lips, I was in disbelief. I retracted my head back in fear and squinted my eyes in confusion.

As he moved in closer, don't tell *a n y o n e*, grabbing the back of my neck and skull firmly with his depraved hands. His tainted, cracked lips pierced mine, his tongue exploring the cavity of my mouth like a shriveled cactus- dirty and dry. I was uncomfortable, to say the least. Although I was aware of my adoration for his attention, I hadn't ever considered moving further in our relationship. I hadn't had a real relationship with anyone.

A few months before this, I had my first kiss with a boy my age in the movie theatres. My first kiss was bashful but exciting; we were both most definitely nervous.

My second kiss caused me to feel torn, back and forth between many directions and deliberate deeply in my mind. I felt like this kiss had been taken from me. I felt responsible because I had enjoyed his attention and money, at first. I found closure in my mind with the fact that it was only a kiss. It could be worse, I shrug. As the nights became longer and winter grew colder, my situation had snowballed, and before I knew it, he was groping me in the back of his black Mercedes. I tell the woman I am working with that night, 'I'm getting a drink from the grocery store down the block, do you want anything?' She declines, but he is waiting for me outside and calls me into his car.

I obey, I have never felt so powerless. Inside of his car, we talk for a little bit, and he tells me a story about a prostitute. He tries to enter me, and I quickly back up into to the door. I say STOP. He whispers don't tell a n y o n e, and I am out, slamming the door as he speeds away. I'm running through the back door of the bakery out of breath and out of my mind.

I was confused before; I didn't think a kiss was a big deal even if it made me feel slightly distressed. I saw it as an annoying chore that I did to get my allowance.

But THIS was clearly not okay. I didn't realize by choosing not to speak up, I was still making a choice, even if it felt easier at the time. My colleague asks what took me so long, I can tell her sensing something is not right, but I awkwardly evade the situation. I was embarrassed and feared she would have blamed me for what was happening. Talking about what was happening would make it real, and I was not ready to accept my reality.

That night when I came home, I created an email address to write about what had happened to me, one that I would never log into again and nobody could ever find. I knew that I needed to get this torture out of me. My attitude has changed from shrugging off the kiss in the back if the bakery. I felt completely to blame. How could I let this happen to me?

I would come home from work every day smelling like sugar and feeling totally violated.

I finally tried to speak out and ask for help. One day after coming home from work and feeling especially dirty, I broke down and was crying on my bathroom floor. At this point, another man who was the delivery driver was taking advantage of me and another friend there. We had talked about it once, and when I asked her what she did, she shrugged her shoulders. Just like me. This delivery driver was much older than me and my friend, I had just entered high school, and she was a year or two older than me. If I had to have guessed how old he was, I would have said maybe thirty; he was forty I found out later. He would use his strength forcibly against me to hold me down and touch me. He would make me touch him, and tell me that I was doing this to him.

It was all my fault.

I am curled up on the mat on the tile floor; I am sobbing so hard I cannot see a foot in front of me. I texted my best friend... she was going to tell her mom, and I panicked. I wished that she did, but I told her I would take care of it. I didn't want my parents to find out; I thought they would be so angry with me. So, I opted for silence, again.

Why the silence? What began as fear and freeze became a part of daily life. Why silence? Why didn't I speak up for myself? Why had I thought it to be more safe hiding rather than confronting what stood before me? I felt the effects of my silence compound over time; the hill could have seemed too high to climb. I felt stuck. I didn't want to admit my initial attraction to these men, I didn't think anyone would understand, and I thought that made it my fault. I thought I knew everything, and that I was supposed to have everything figured out. I thought everyone would have seen me as perverted and that I got the love and attention I was so desperately seeking.

A few months later, I decided to confide in a boyfriend. I dated two boys while this was happening. The first boyfriend I was able to muster the courage to send him a text one night, 'my boss is molesting me.' I was met with silence, and we never talked about it. The second boyfriend, I had been lying to, I told him about the delivery driver's abuse, and he hated him with a burning passion and would threaten to go inside and physically harm him, but he never did. No one knew what to do, or how to speak up.

I started using drugs, really anything that I could find to take my focus off of this torture when this began. Being in an altered state felt like a release, but it was just an escape from my living nightmare. My use began with smoking pot in the woods behind the high school, and going to different people's houses to get high. Quickly, I became introduced to all different types of drugs, which I was paying for using the extra money that the old man gave me. I enjoyed morphine, Adderall, cocaine, and ecstasy.

I would alternate depending on availability and take them in school or at night when my parents were asleep. I felt cool because I was hanging out with older people and found a way to escape my pain. I was even smiling, and having fun in my regular life. And they were making me skinny too. I remember Adderall always lasting longer than the school day; I would come home and not be hungry for dinner.

The cocaine use was enhanced with my first boyfriend. I would walk to his house, sometimes it would just be us, or sometimes our friends were there too. We would make some phone calls, get some cocaine, flip his grandmother's photo on his wall over and have fun.

We would go on walks, relax, and in these times, I felt like a free flower. This was my first real relationship with another human besides these two older men, even though it was based on drugs, it felt very real. When I would use in school, sometimes I would snort alone and sometimes with a friend or two. We would go to the bathroom; I would have it all ready, so we could just break out some lines on my pocket Sephora mirror, in two minutes we were in heaven. One time I and another girl were in a stall together, suddenly we hear a 'knock, knock' it's the security guard, and my stomach drops.

We quickly lick the mirror and exit, telling them that we needed help with feminine hygiene. They did NOT believe us at all, but once being brought to the dean's office and bringing up my records, they saw that I was in all honors classes and hadn't really had any prior trouble. I was always good at school, learning and tests have always come easily to me. Got off free, go me.

My prayers were finally answered when I was thoroughly fed up and quit. I stayed through for two years of abuse. I moved on to another job and to this day, I reflect on why I stayed at this bakery for so long.

My story speaks to the amount of helplessness a human can feel and has inspired me to live with more compassion towards myself and others. For so long; I lived behind a fake smile and blue eyes that saw planet earth as an ugly world. My experience has allowed me to understand that a person can be going through so much and not be able to talk about it with anyone. Everyone's eyes have seen a different past, they have read a different story. To struggle is to be human, our pain unites us, forming strong bonds with others in the circles of our lives.

The end of this abuse is the dawn of my different life. When I left the bakery, I never wanted to think about this again... being completely incapable of coping with my abuse and integrate these events into my consciousness caused me to suppress these emotions, burying them deeper and deeper, until one day, I forgot.

I forgot everything. I could not synthesize this suffering into my life, the life that everyone saw me in. The life that everyone believed me to have.

The life that I fought so hard to hold up.

I wish I could recognize the amount of psychological torture and emotional trauma this was putting me through and how fast my wounds would amplify in the future.

My veil was lifted several years later. I was no longer taking drugs but had developed severely disordered eating. My eating disorder began at a young age, around the time I began cutting myself. When I was thirteen and felt the pressures of 'looking good' and being skinny. My perception of myself was already tainted with self-hatred, and now I had another lens to pick myself apart through. I remember the first time I purged a meal, I had just binged on chocolate ice-cream, and no one was home.

I am so guilty, creeping up the stairs to my bathroom and lifting up the toilet seat as I crouch down. I think disgusting thoughts and fumble around my mouth with my fingers until I feel something happening inside of me. A constriction and then an upheaval, the ice cream has yet to merge with the inside of my body, so it feels cool as it comes back up and pours into the toilet.

Phew, I feel better.

I continued down this path of self-disciplined torture for several years. In university, my diet was completely out of control, I would go through cycles of eating very little, to eating every single thing I could get my hands on in one breath. So much that my stomach would hurt I would pass out from tiredness of feeling this way, wake up and binge again. Starving and binging because a cycle that escalated once I left schooling and entered adulthood. As life ebbs and flows, so did my eating.

I hit a particularly low point when I looked at myself in the mirror and couldn't believe what I had created. I was now twenty pounds heavier than when I finished school six months ago, and was so ashamed, even though I was actually at a normal, healthy weight. I had no job, no money, no boyfriend and moved back in with my parents. Although I was twenty-one years old, I had a vague sense that this was a very difficult point in my life, a sort of rock-bottom.

I hadn't been in a relationship for a while and was so desperately craving human connection.

The beautiful moments slowly arising as the sun blooms to the morning, feeling the breath of your lover steadily tingling the hairs on your neck with your warm shared air. The connection of having someone who cares and loves you.

Someone to appreciate, and to make you laugh. Someone to smile with. Someone to spend time with, and grow with.

I was kidnapped by the driver of my cab on my way home from a horrible date. The date was in Williamsburg, at his place and I wanted us to work out so badly. He was wealthy by his own terms, a real estate investor, young, handsome, and foreign. I didn't feel good enough for him. I never actually felt good enough for anyone, which explains why I spent time with men that would raise the volume on the television when I started talking. I feel like I have to do backbends to be seen. The night was getting late, and he had to be awake early the next morning. Initially, I had hoped he would ask me to stay over but by the flow of conversation, rather a lack thereof, I saw that was not where this was going.

In a huff, I put on my coat to storm out, and he pulls me back in, 'let me get you a car...' the cabdriver 'misunderstood' me when I gave him my address.

I am not paying attention to my surroundings because I am fuming about my lousy date until I come to my senses and feel disoriented. I know the way home, and this is NOT it. The buildings don't even look the same, where are we? The driver thought I wanted him to take me to dinner and then back to his house in New Jersey. I start screaming. And then crying, it was the first time I had cried in a while. It was at this point I really had to look at myself and figure out what I was doing to attract this situation in my life. I was staying in Battery Park City that winter, as the cab driver returned me home, dripping in tears and sweat, I take the elevator uppppp, plop into bed after a breakdown in the shower, open my journal and write... the story of the bakery comes pouring out of my fingers and I breakdown some more after realizing for the first time in my life I was molested. How could I not have understood what was happening?

And then, how could I forget, really, how could I forget something so horrible... it didn't make sense to me at the time, but I felt the pain of my past worse than ever before.

I close my eyes again. I see darkness; I see patterns, I see swirling colors. I am brought back to last summer, on my yoga mat at Satya Yoga Shala. Lying in a cool, shadowy Savasana, corpse pose. In this posture, the body does nothing but rest, allowing maximum absorption of all the delicious benefits of asana practice. Asana is the part of yoga that is the postures, the dynamic movements. Yoga is a lifestyle, a mindset and way of being. Some other parts of yoga include breathing exercises, kindness, truthfulness, and meditation. Practicing Asana has shifted my entire perspective. Through yoga, I have become more in tune with my body, and thus in tune with the pain that was present here.

These profound wounds that I had suppressed for five years had rooted their way into my subconscious until I found a way of coping with my experience. Yoga is my coping, and my healing. By relaxing my body, I have relaxed my mind. The body stores trauma within every cell if we are not able to integrate it immediately.

Through the practice of Asana, as I released deeper into each posture and shifted my focus to healing and anchoring more love, light, and grace to myself, the people around me, and the global community. I began feeling amazing changes in my mind state and wellbeing. I was not only paying attention to myself, my thoughts, and feelings - I heard the story start to change. Day by day, I was noticing my thoughts become kind and more gentle, from becoming frustrated and anxious, taking things personally, to more at peace, understanding, and loving. Yoga was the most important key in my healing journey, and has truly helped me in so many ways.

Beginning was not easy; I started taking short, beginner classes on Youtube and wouldn't be able to finish some of them, I would get so tired and frustrated and beat myself up with my words. And then magically, one day I was able to do something that I wasn't able to do the day before. Since that day, I have continued my practice. I expanded my practice to yoga studio classes when I felt confident and able to do some basic postures.

A year and a half into my practice, the opportunity of teacher training emerged, and my subconscious sang YES. This 200hr teacher training has also been a further step into healing from my past traumas. It was one of the most difficult things I had to do. Since graduating, I do not teach classes but know that I will when I am ready.

Yoga is not a sport for me; yoga is a sacred, safe space to explore and define our personal boundaries. What I learn from myself on my mat carries over into my life off of my mat, because yoga is truly a way of life for me.

The end of class, I lay in stillness. Savasana, corpse pose... I attempt to focus on my breath, releasing and relaxing into the present moment allowing gravity to assist my body in settling in... my mind is racing, replaying the visions in my mind of memories of a time when I really hated myself. What to do with this concentrated and confused inner turmoil? I begin to sense the disconnect between my body and mind. Everything that happened to me felt like an attack, my walls were up, and I was guarding my castle from every single pore. It hurts. It's exhausting. It's sometimes scary.

These images flashed through my mind, and I would try my best to not react on them, not get twisted into a story that was so personal and hurt me so much. I am disconnecting myself from the experience because it is no longer a part of me. Letting go of what no longer serves me. I inhale deeply, trying to release... and I give up. Like a rubber band snapping, after it has reached its threshold, my mind gives up and my body contorts, shrieking with grief and allowing the pain to consume me. I was in a safe space, I had no idea what was happening, but I knew I couldn't fight it anymore.

To Sal and Tony -

This letter for you is difficult for me to write because I hate thinking about you. I have tried, unsuccessfully, to never think of you again. To shut out the pain, to blockade you from my head and my heart. I cannot run from my subconscious mind. I cannot run from fate. Thinking about the pain causes me to relive the experience in my bones. Talking about it makes it real, and I wish more than anything that this was all some sort of twisted nightmare. If only our lives had different paths, the torture that would have been spared. The countless nights of crying, jumping out of my skin, and the absolute fear of intimacy and dozens of failed relationships. The emotions shattered like broken glass, reflecting the bleeding mascara running down my face on the subway ride home. The isolation. The deep isolation. All of it, gone, if only I hadn't known you. I feel so alone because of this, and because of you. You make me feel like a monster. I want you to know that I'M NOT OKAY. I don't know if I'll ever be okay, and that makes me want to fucking die. I am still angry. I am still living in fear of others.

I still feel the pain, even though it has been almost ten years since you changed my life forever. You have affected every part of me. I am choosing to hold on to this grief. This misery and heartbreak are mines now, and I will take care of them like children until they are ready to travel the universe unaccompanied by my body.

...

In the moments when this desolation departs from me, I rise. Without this experience, I would not have gone searching for and come back with the genuine appreciation for being okay. For living just one moment without pain, without worry, and without fear. Without you, I would not have found my self-esteem, and I would not have found MY VOICE. I would not have found my strength.

My He. Art.

Petra Flora

Snared

Daily through the disturbed ripples of hot debates, one hears the broad versions of domestic violence and rape, by the professionals who know, by those who know very little, and by those who have absolutely no clue of what they are talking about. Due to this, the essential subject of educating every level of society about the physical, emotional and spiritual dangers and setbacks of domestic violence and rape remains extremely limited.

Without a doubt, ignorance plays a major role in the changing pattern of human behaviour today. Where most females only realise the serious implications of these violent crimes after they have fallen victim to it. Even with all the warning against these violent crimes are passed onto the public by various social and media networks, the problem of ignorance remains a major concern. The only outcome is that the majority of females today still actually refuse to believe that any one of these violent crimes could happen to them. As a survivor of domestic violence and rape, I also refused to believe in the reality of becoming a victim, which also almost cost me my life.

This is my story. My most painful story. My true story.

South Africa. 1980.

In the year of 1980 there was no formal rape information or educational system in place, and being ignorant about the dangers of rape was common.

I was at a friend's house when I met a young man named Shawn. He came forward as charming with a neat appearance, everything about him seemed to impress me. My thoughts and actions exaggerating everything good thing I could ever think of a human being. He was it. After the visit at my friend's home, he offered to take me home, and I with pure intentions invited him in for a cup of coffee. My parents were asleep already, and their bedroom door was closed. Shawn who I was utterly impressed with, whom I stared at with the excitement of a child. An innocent disbelief that humans this good even existed, until he started touching me. His hands all over my breasts.

I told him to stop.

Stop.

With my heart racing and fear escaping violently from the pores of my skin, he refused and roughly pulled me down onto the floor, telling me to not make a sound.

With a strong force, he overpowered me and there I was at the tender age of fifteen. Viciously raped in my own home by a young man I believed I could trust. With a charming facade, he ensnared me and imposed his absolute power on me so that my personality was systematically destroyed, resulting in complete subjection. My cries of: "Please. NO." These words fell on deaf ears, and I was forced to watch the grunting smirk on his face while he satisfied his sexual lust.

The roots of sadism. Sadism. The act of deriving sexual satisfaction from inflicting pain, either physical or mental has many causes, including an inability to cope with feelings of shame associated with sex, hostility towards parents or other figures of authority, and feelings of inferiority.

Although there seems to be an abyss separating the 'normal' male instinct and the sadist's desire to inflict pain, the two spring from the same root. In its simplest form, the male sexual impulse is impersonal, focused on a desire to 'do something' to the partner; the act of penetration is in itself a kind of aggression.

He, Shawn then left and took every part of my being with him. Hurt. Humiliated and ashamed to the innermost parts of my core. Deeply afraid of telling my parents, and what their reaction might be. With rape being a family disgrace at the time, I was filled, overflowing with extreme hurt and fear, covered with guilt. Humiliation and shame were so close it comforted me, being afraid of telling my parents or reporting it to the relevant authorities.

This most violent sexual attack was not only against my body, but it was also against my sense of autonomy as well. Being a pathetic attack of so-called power and dominance, the rape was highly devastating to me. My parents could only give limited support during the crises period. They were loving, understanding, kind, compassionate and caring. But their love and compassion could not heal the scars.

The extensive damage this sexual crime inflicted on my sense of personal integrity, dramatically interfered with my fragile personal identity and sense of self-esteem that were being forged during this period.

With the refusal to report the rape, the refusal to be shamed by an act my community would not accept.

I had daily encounters with the perpetrator who was in the same school as I was. There was no escaping; I could not even escape his shadow. This inability to make such a human disappear. With anger dramatically added to my sense of shame and humiliation, complicating my trauma pattern extensively.

Between 1990 and 2002, I had met the man who would become my husband. At first, his exterior showed forth a desirable charm; he was respectful and helpful. His charm held no boundaries; it was infinite extending towards all people and in all things. Yes. Again, ignorance became the snare.

But just as fast as night became day, things changed. In the early stage of our marriage, I started noticing a side of him I did not know. And there it began, my repugnant and resentful runway to hell. He started drinking a lot and became extremely controlling and aggressive, putting a lot of fear and pressure on my life, weighing me down.

Because he is Afrikaans speaking and I am English speaking, he loved humiliating me before his family, the joke of the family, calling me all types of dirty names.

One thing was clear since the beginning of this ill matrimony between woman and man. His family saw me as an intruder and treated me like one. I had invaded the wrong life, a life that would swallow me whole.

As a married woman and a supposed intruder. I experienced a most traumatic and fearful life with a man who was an alcoholic and a monstrous abuser. Who turned me into a punching bag, a floor rag and a slave on a regular basis.

Many times, in drunken rage he, my so-called husband accused me falsely, heaven only knows the things that poisoned his mind. The demons dancing around in his skull possessed him to do the most unnatural things. Causing him to hit me and point his firearm at my head, threatening to kill me if I ever spoke out or tried to leave him. I was turned into an animal by a human.

As an aggressive man, a man loyal to his violence, he showed me no remorse or regret and was unconcerned about my rights and feelings as a woman and as his wife. The unbreakable fear of death was now constantly banging against the inside of my head, a cloud heavy over my head.

My thoughts had been overtaken with reason. What does he see in me? The man I married. Was he always, this? Have I become the nightmare he was unable to wake from?

I no longer recall the rays of sun that lit up our wedding day. The breeze floating through my dress. They had all become distant memories.

The one thing that I never questioned or reasoned with was that I believed it was safer not to speak out or report the ongoing domestic violence to anyone. I chose to do what I thought would save my life. I chose to remain silent. To allow every ounce of hurt to become nothing but ghosts.

Feeling trapped in a web of destruction, the more I tried to break free from this deadly web, the more I was beaten and threatened. With this, I lost all hope and respect for myself, my marriage and my ex-husband. No longer human. Like a slave, I did exactly what he ordered me to do, and I felt sickened when on-demand he had sex with me, making love never existed.

There were many nights that he would push me out of the house for hours in the cold of the night, leaving me to sink deep into my emotions of feeling powerless, afraid, helpless, cold, hungry and angry.

I always prayed to God for help. With my eyes fixed on the heavens. These were times when I sincerely prayed the hardest, always fearing what was going to happen next. To emotionally hurt me further, to strengthen his abusive power over me, and to scare me. He took his firearm and killed my dogs, in one firm loud gesture saying: "This will happen to you if you ever disobeyed him." The creatures I once loved, were lifeless, gone as if they never were.

In this sickening, abusive marriage we had three sons. Three beautiful boys. My peace and my reasons to live. Every pregnancy filled me with many mixed emotions, but it also gave me hope that things might get better in our marriage. He was kind but not lovable, and very strict with our three sons. My three sons who were still very young at the time, witnessed many times how my ex-husband would swear at me, beat me up and threaten me with his firearm. My sons feared their father and would always run and hide when he physically and emotionally abused me. Again, a quick gaze at the heavens, making sure God knows that I am speaking to Him. I feared what they'd become, that what they were living would ruin their lives.

That the same merciless demons that lived in their father would start dancing around in their souls.

My sons and I were very close to each other, and they always opened up to me about problems, these were the time I felt most normal. The domestic violence, however, did have an extremely bad effect on their school education, and their personality and character formation.

With my last pregnancy, I had a miscarriage due to being beaten up by my ex-husband. It was a girl, which I so much wanted, and even today I still wonder with tears how wonderful she would have now been. What colour her eyes would have held, the sound of her laughter ringing in the house. The pain in her tears that only the love of a mother could comfort. I'll never know. It felt as though I had lost a most precious part of my life, which until this day makes me think a lot about the little girl I so viciously lost.

A deep hurt difficult to conquer.

Due to my miscarriage, I moved into the spare bedroom of our home, but this did not stop the physical and emotional abuse from my ex-husband, it just got worse.

In 2002 the time arrived when I just could not take the abuse and threats any longer, and I told my ex-husband, "I am moving out and leaving you for good." In a drunken rage, he went to his gun safe and took out his hunting rifle and loaded it. My ears sensitive to every move he was making, loading his rifle, his harsh footsteps on the ground. All loud in my ears. Deafening. Shouting that he is going to now kill me. As he had gestured with the killing of my dogs, I was about to become what he promised I would be. Dead. Out of fear I shouted to my three young sons to go and lock themselves in their bedroom upstairs.

One of my sons hid under his bed that night. My eldest son ran upstairs and hid in the room, and my youngest son was just a few meters ahead of me on the stairway, calling to me with desperation, crying his heart out in fear, telling me to hurry up.

My second eldest son was forced to stand next to my ex-husband, and he was begging his father to please stop.

I stopped to look where my second eldest son was and saw him standing at the bottom of the stairway next to my ex-husband pleading with him not to shoot me.

I saw my ex-husband aim his hunting rifle straight at me, certain that this was it. I was going to become part of the Earth that everyone so freely walks on and neglects at the same time. The next thing I heard was a shot go off. I felt terrible pain, and I fell to the floor rolling down the stairway. Blood flowing from my face, lower back and hips as I lay on the floor at the bottom of the stairway. Calling out for help from my three sons. I saw my ex-husband walk out the front door with his hunting rifle and I heard another shot go off.

My youngest son was sitting on the stairway, and I asked him to fetch my cell-phone from my room and bring it to me, which he did, with great courage. With my hands, full of blood, I pushed the button of my contact list on my cell phone, and it was my ex-husband's brother's wife that answered on the other side. Now in and out of consciousness due to the loss of blood and shock, I told my ex-husband's brother's wife what had happened, and the next thing I knew was that I was surrounded by paramedics. The one paramedic told me that I am lucky to still be alive, as the bullet of my ex-husband's hunting rifle hit the railing of the stairway and its pieces of shrapnel deeply penetrated parts of my face, my lower back and my hips.

They put me on a stretcher, loaded me into an ambulance and rushed me to the nearest hospital. The only place I could look was up. Did God see all the lunacy, will He save me?

I was taken to the emergency section where the doctor stitched the wounds in my face, put a drip on me and gave me a sedative injection for my pain and condition of shock.

The next thing I remember was waking up in a hospital ward, lying in a bed soaked in my own blood. My mother, father and sister were standing next to my bed, their faces vague but highly upset. My sister went to the ward sister and asked her why I was lying in a bed soaked with blood and why have the doctors not treated my lower back and hip wounds from the shooting.

The ward sister told my sister, that I was not a priority patient and that I will just have to wait for my turn.

After lying in the blood-soaked bed in the ward for almost 24 hours, they took me into a theatre to repair the damage the shrapnel did to my lower back and hips.

The next morning when I woke up, the doctor who operated on me, told me that he could not remove the shrapnel of the bullet, as it was too deeply embedded in my muscle tissues, and it would cause greater damage to my lower back and hips. After the doctor had left, I needed to use the toilet, and I discovered I could not walk on my own. Even though God spared my life. More than ever I felt I was dying, slowly. This was when the ward sister brought me a walker to walk with, and in great pain, I burst out in tears. What has my life become?

During my week stay in the hospital, I had to learn how to walk with crutches, which was extremely upsetting to me, and a lot of anger built up inside of me because of the damage my ex-husband so violently bestowed upon me. What I did not know at the time, is that the investigating officer's responsibility was to come and take a statement of the shooting from me while I was in the hospital, which he did not do. I did not have my cell-phone with me, and I could not contact my three young sons to find out whether they are fine and safe. All this, just aggravated my Post Traumatic Stress Disorder to a great extent.

What I also did not know, is that the doctor who treated my wounds was legally responsible for writing a full report of my wounds and my emotional condition for the Police report, which he did not do. I also did not receive any form of trauma counselling at the hospital, which would have been most beneficial in my case against my husband.

What I was not further aware of, is the fact that the blood-stained clothes that I had on, on the night of the shooting was to be put into a plastic bag and handed over to the forensic department as evidence in the case of attempted murder against my ex-husband, and that photos were also to be taken of the crime scene. This was not done, and the blood-stained clothes with the holes of the shrapnel that I had on was thrown away. Not knowing anything about the Legal system at the time or my legal rights as the victim, ignorance became the snare, and my ex-husband still had the power to manipulate me and the legal system.

On the day of my discharge from the hospital for safety reasons and to recover from my painful wounds, I went and stayed with my father and mother. Once there, I phoned my ex-husband's brother's wife to find out about my three sons.

Rudely she told me that she is taking care of them and cut me off.

Was this the purpose of my creation? To be cut off, to be abused and slowly lose my sanity.

I immediately phoned a good friend of mine and asked her if she would pick up my three sons and take care of them for a while until I have recovered from the wounds.
She agreed with haste and fetched my three sons from my ex-husband's brother's home, me not knowing at the time, that my good friend and my ex-husband was having an affair. I now believe, that she was feeding my ex-husband with all the information about my problem, which I shared with her confidentially. How did I not see that? She was always willing, willing to help, almost too zealous for my liking.

A flawed investigation and lack of forensic tests, allowed my ex-husband to walk free from a charge of attempted murder.

Was bribery and defeating the ends of justice the cause of this?

Three weeks of staying with my father and mother, I still heard nothing from the Investigating Officer, and I did not even know the name of the Investigating Officer. My sister agreed to take me through to the Police Station that was closest to where the violent crime was committed, and at the Police Station, it took me over an hour to find an Investigating Officer who knew about the shooting. I told him that I would like to lay a charge of attempted murder against my ex-husband, and rudely he took my statement with a forceful irritation, which I signed. I then asked the Investigating Officer where my ex-husband was, and he told me that my ex-husband was locked up in the Police Cells. Again, not knowing, that the Investigating Officer was supposed to give me a case number, which he did not do.

I also discovered later on that the Investigating Officer lied to me, by telling me that my ex-husband was locked up at the Police Station because no one can be detained for longer than 48 hours without being charged with a crime.
Before any person can be charged with a crime, a full statement is required from the victim, and my statement was only taken four weeks after the crime was committed.

This gives a clear indication that some type of bribery and defeating the ends of justice was taking place with this attempted murder case.

Having no income, my sister helped me find a flat and paid three months of rent in advance for me until I found a suitable job. Helping me with some furniture and getting me back on my feet. I then was able to get my three sons and move into the flat. Two weeks later I found a job, and my three sons attended a school close by. We were happy to be together again and shared a lot of happy moments. It was about three weeks after this when I received a phone call from the Investigating Officer, who informed me that my ex-husband is out on bail, but what he did not tell me, is that my ex-husband was legally not allowed to see or come into contact with me at all. At the same time, it seemed as if though a light was starting to peep through, gently touching my life. The heavens must have heard something.

A week later there was a knock at my front door, and when I opened the door, my ex-husband pushed me out of the way and entered my flat, entered my life, demanding to see our three sons.

And dark clouds once again covered the bit of light that started touching my life. Filled with extreme fear and not knowing what to do, I let him see our boys.

Our.

The mere thought of sharing something with this man, sent shivers down my spine, caused the hair on my skin to stand erect. These visits carried on for about four weeks, where my ex-husband would arrive smelling of alcohol and verbally abuse me, calling me a bitch, a whore and other names that fed his ego and sense of authority. Perhaps my once good friend had shared too much information with him.

One early morning while making breakfast for my three sons, the evil force, my ex-husband just burst into my flat, started pushing me around and swearing at me. He threatened that he was going to take our boys away from me, saying that he will see to it that I land up in the gutters. Through all this, I just could not take it anymore and broke down. The artifice of light that touched my life vanished.

When my ex-husband left, I called my good friend and told her what had happened, and if she could please take care of my three sons while I go see a doctor at the hospital. Strangely enough, as though she knew and that all was well planned because she gladly accepted. Elize was always very friendly, always asked questions. Which I believed was showing concern, and she was always over willing to take care of the boys. Now this reason is clear.

I dropped my three sons off at my supposed to be '*good friend*' I only found out about my friend Elize and my ex-husband when I was admitted for mental health treatment. She was feeding him with all the confidential information I foolishly shared with her. Nonetheless, I went straight to the hospital where they previously treated me for my wounds. In a traumatised state I saw a doctor and explained what had happened.

The doctor immediately got hold of an ambulance, filled out forms and told me that he is having me admitted to a mental hospital for evaluation and treatment, because of my emotional state.

Whether I entirely comprehended the grave nature of being admitted to a mental hospital. I will never know.

The mental hospital was very formal, strict, almost prison-like, very stressful and scary, especially to any new patient. Even though I was in an open ward, at night, we were locked up until 6 am the next morning. Not being used to such an environment, makes one's life most unpleasant. Overly sensitive to silence, as the shooting remains a haunting and tormenting ghost of the past. Each time I heard a bang around me, fear filled my heart, and I see the whole picture of the shooting replay itself before my eyes. Uninvited it would appear, and I was back on the stairway, about to lose my life and my boys.

During my three week stay at the Mental Hospital, I was heavily sedated and was also informed by my employer that I no longer have a job. Once again having no cell phone or money, I could not contact the Investigating Officer, or my parents and children. Now without a job, I lost the flat, and I was completely shattered, that I was kept under heavy observation.

My *good friend* knew I was admitted to a Mental Hospital, but yet made no effort to bring my three sons to visit me. Was she too busy enjoying things that were never hers? Making a life of peace out of my darkness for herself.

The Investigating Officer who also knew my good friend made no effort in contacting me and letting me know what progress was made with the attempted murder case.

Two days before I was discharged from the Mental Hospital, still heavily sedated, I was called in by the psychiatrist who was treating me, and he informed me that I suffer from a mental illness known as Bipolar stage 2 and severe Post Traumatic Stress Disorder. He further informed me that as I have no income and that I have lost my flat, that they arranged for me to stay at a private Care Center. That's not the best of it, he further informed me that I qualify for a Government disability grant, which is not much, but it will help me pay my rent at the Care Center. A rollercoaster of highs and lows.

The good came with the bad.

Then the shocking news came when the Psychiatrist told me to withdraw the attempted murder case against my ex-husband, as it will only cause greater damage. As previously mentioned, at the time I was ignorant about the Legal procedures and my rights as the victim, I only found out much later, that the Psychiatrist had no right to tell me to withdraw the attempted murder case against my ex-husband, and that it was his legal responsibility to recommend a professional social worker to be with me at every Court hearing of the case. The other problem was, the Psychiatrist told me this while I was heavily sedated and he knew I could not think clearly.

On the day of my discharge from the Mental Hospital, my supposed to be *good friend* picked me up and took me to the Police Station to see the Investigating Officer. I told the Investigating Officer what the Psychiatrist told me about withdrawing the attempted murder case against my ex-husband, and more than willing he said it was fine, and that the case will be withdrawn.

Later on, through doing research and study on cases such as mine, I discovered that once someone is charged with a serious crime, the case can only be withdrawn in a Court of Law by the Magistrate in the presence of the accused and the complainant. The case was no longer in the hands of the Investigating Officer but was in the hands of the Prosecuting Authority, and therefore, the Investigating Officer had no authority to withdraw my case of attempted murder against my husband.

Based on five different Legal experts I approached with my 70-page statement, they all confirm that the attempted murder case against my ex-husband was illegally withdrawn and is thus still an open case. The light has favour on me once again. They further confirmed, that the whole Investigating procedure of this case by not being given a case number, was full of unjust flaws and that for some reason and in some way, I was deceived through the whole investigating procedure and abused by the Justice System.

Not once was I notified by the Investigating Officer or the Court of any dates of the Court case hearings and not once was I given the opportunity to attend any of the Court Case hearings, which was legally my right as the victim to know of Court dates and hearings.

This was a serious violation of my rights as the victim of a serious violent crime.

As advised by the Legal experts, I contacted the Independent Complaints Commission of the South African Police Services, the National Prosecuting Authority and the Justice Department, but for the past, ongoing five years now, I just do not get any replies from them. The Legal experts told me that they are refusing to respond because they know they messed up and are afraid of a certainly strong Civil Law Suit that can be made against the State.

Unfortunately, they are all more than willing and prepared to take my case, but with me being on a small disability grant, I cannot afford the Legal fees. The upsetting thing about this matter is that victims of Domestic Violence and Sexual Assault do not get free access to Attorneys, whereas the perpetrators have the right to free Legal representation in Court and have the right to receive bail, so just to victimize their victims directly or indirectly. This confirms the fact, that women do not have equal rights to men, even when it is claimed they do. It is a statement people make to make us feel better for a moment. That for a split second we exist and are of great importance.

After being discharged from the Mental Hospital and after seeing the Investigation Officer, I went to the Care Center as referred to the Psychiatrist. Arriving there It felt as if everything started all over again feeling afraid, hurt, angry and lonely because the Care Center did not allow children. With my disturbing disadvantaged situation, my ex-husband through his Attorney gave me no option, and I had to sign my three sons over into his care. My ex-husband's words to me were; "I told you I'd drive you down into the gutters." He was successful, and the demons in his brain now rejoiced fervently.

During my stay at the Care Center, the single women were always manipulated by single sex starved men. One night the Leader and his friend of the Care Center came to my room and started to chat with me. The Leader came and sat on my bed next to me and put his hand just above my knee. He then put his hand on my breast and said he and his friend would like to have sex with me. I pushed his hands off my body, and before I could stand up and run out of the room, he and his friend pushed me down on the bed, pulled down my pants and their pants. The Leader climbed on top of me, and while his friend held my hands, he raped me.

When he was finished, he told his friend, that it was his turn. After this most sickening and frightening violent attack, they walked out of my room laughing, warning me that they will have me kicked out of the Care Center should I try and report them. If the mind was a colour, mine was black.

Pitch black.

The Care Center, if one can call it that, which is similar to the mental hospital, and was not an easy going comfortable place to stay at. There were people, male and female of different walks of life, many being rough, rude and rebellious. We were not allowed off the premises without permission and were forced to do daily chores, and if not done we were punished.

The next day I approached the owner of the Care Center who is a Pastor, and I tearfully told her what had happened. Her answer was that I must keep quiet about the sexual attack, as it will damage the Care Center's and her reputation, which will also stop the donations the Care Center receives.

Be quiet.

All I ever did, the only thing I knew.

A few months later being torn, hurting and lonely, I had a talk with the Head Monitor of the Care Center. The Head Monitor, of the Care Center at that time, did National child, woman abuse and sexual assault. Road show awareness campaigns for over 16 years before he came to the Care Center. He successfully worked with well over 3700 victims of these crimes and ran his own 24/7 crises clinic.

He was the only one who saw my pain and my fear, and this made it easy for me to open up to him and tell him everything, even about the rape at the Care Center. After months, we fell deeply in love with each other, and we got married, and this was when he took me out of the Care Center, now we live peacefully in our own space, right next door to the hospital where I receive my monthly treatment.

The light was bright on my life finally.

As my ex-husband and I got divorced in 2003, the Head Monitor and I eventually got married in 2011. I could finally start stitching up wounds, wounds I pray nobody will ever be able to open again.

We found an affordable small garden flat and moved out of the Care Center, where we have been staying for four years now. As my husband is on an old age pension grant and I receive a disability grant, we pay our monthly rent first, and with the little money we have left we can barely survive. It's always easier surviving when you are filled with a healthy and true kind of love.

Psychologically and spiritually, this most sickening violent rape attack became a vicious ghost, that aggressively haunts me until this day. I have become extremely sensitive to sexual related issues, and when I am approached in a wrong way by any man, I become highly upset.
Because I have now learned, that there are a high number of men, that go beyond the limits of risk to reach their goal when it comes to overpowering women to have sex.

Even with the best precautions in place, every adult, adolescent and even younger females remain a potential rape victim today. Not arising from any particular race, age, or income group, all rapists are out to create fear and destroy not only the lives of their victims but also the lives of the victim's family.

Without a doubt, that which we know about the increase of sexual crimes, we refuse to accept the reality of the physical, psychological and spiritual dangers and setbacks of sexual crimes.

Based upon International case files and statistical reports on domestic violence, it remains an undisputed fact within social circles today, that domestic violence is rapidly on the increase.

Due to the lack of effective preventative and intervention platforms in many of the Countries, ignorance once again becomes the snare for the victims. It is here where Government Officials, Psychiatrists, Psychologists and Sociologists throughout the World are continuously finding themselves facing new aggressive behavioural patterns within every society, making it extremely difficult to stop the powerful flow of domestic violence. As a result of this, there is no doubt that the spiritual dangers and the psychological setbacks of victims are becoming more and more complicated, which frustrates valuable therapy procedures.

Undeniably this does create a major problem within the modern trends of every society, whereas with rape victims, so too with domestic violence victims are being misunderstood, misjudged, ignored and even silenced on a regular basis. Due to this, with highly disturbed emotions of guilt, shame, resentment, humiliation, hurt and fear, pent-up frustration normally becomes the victim's choice of not speaking out. Clearly noticeable, the choice of not speaking out aggravates the victim's character degradation and personality disorganisation that was forcefully and painfully forged during the violent attack or attacks.

To simplify this unwanted character and personality formation that was brutally initiated by domestic violence, the spiritual values and the mental abilities of victims basically become captured and bound by the merciless hands of the perpetrators. Unseen to the naked eye, this gives a painful, unwanted birth to victims of tormenting ghosts, who inexorably haunt the victims on a continuous basis. With fear being the main contributing factor, the prognosis of this in Psychological terms is known as Post Traumatic Stress Disorder, which also leads to spiritual oppression.

This does substantiate the fact that all victims of domestic violence and sexual assault do require immediate attention from highly qualified and professional physical, mental and spiritual health services.

The importance is, victims of Domestic Violence and Sexual Assault need to always seek professional legal advice and to know exactly how the Investigation procedure works, and what their rights as victims are. Because as in my case, this is how ignorance becomes a deadly snare for many females, with no return for any type of mental or spiritual cure.

Once a cup is broken, no matter how well one patches that cup together again, the cracks always show and the cup can never be the same again.

To this day, I still see a Psychiatrist and Psychologist at our local Government hospital once a month, which will go on for years to come, and as I also suffer from acute asthma, I also see the lung clinic at the hospital once a month. The shrapnel in my hips and lower back has shifted deeper into the muscle tissues hitting some of the nerves.

I cannot sit for longer than 15 minutes at a time and cannot walk long distances. The doctors say that the shrapnel cannot be removed as it could cause me to become paralyzed from my lower back down.

Being that my children are now adults and that my ex-husband walked away as a free man after almost killing me, he has brainwashed them, making them believe that I am the guilty one and that I deliberately signed them off in 2003. Now I have lost my three sons too, as my ex-husband has bought their trust with gifts and free food and accommodation, knowing I cannot compete with this.

Today with my sons being adults, there seems to be a major communication gap. Only my youngest and second eldest sons communicate with me now and then, the eldest son for some unknown reason has cut me off completely. I have tried so many times to bond with them, but it seems they are blaming me for everything that has gone wrong in our lives. The only thing left, is for me to pray for them and hold onto the hope I have left.

Within the twelve years of this most abusive marriage, I believe with all the tears that flowed from my eyes; I could have filled many rivers.

Five Legal experts have confirmed that bribery and defeating the ends of justice was the ticket for my ex-husband to walk out free from a violent crime that he committed. This also clearly shows the signs of a psychopathic personality on my ex-husband's side, who is an extremely good emotional disguise artist with grossly abnormal responses.

Through my ignorance, lack of support, counselling and my vulnerability, I became entrapped in a deadly web of manipulation and deceit, which dragged me into the vicious hands of a double rape

To the person that was there for me at every turn of the road. Early mornings and late nights. The person who still gets up at 2 AM twice a month to get my medication for me. To the man who has worked with women and children who have been abused, molested and sexually assaulted for over 20 years. If it were not for him, I would have never made it. To my husband of six years. Thank you.

This is my story. My most painful story. This is my strength, my passion for survival. This is my true story.

Inside The Box

Boxes.

Boxes everywhere...

Some small... Some large... Some square shaped... Some round... Some even seem untouched, whereas others are ruined at the corners, tiny holes where only the tiniest of existence could have entered. Some boxes are taped shut while others are wound and tied closed with twine.

I sit on the cold wood floor, legs crossed and folded into each other. A soft wool blanket is hugged over my shoulders and tucked under my knees trapping the heat from my body to keep me warm. I sit tightly holding onto myself and just stare at the boxes that surround me. It's like they are glaring back at me, beckoning me to lift their lids for a quick peak. Begging for a moment of attention. Inanimate objects which now sound like children playing in a park. "Pick me! Pick me!" Not sure how I've gotten to the point where I am fully capable of ignoring the screams coming from the boxes. It must be all the years I have taught myself to compartmentalize. I have perfected the art of storing memories, nightmares, feelings and emotions tightly into individually wrapped boxes.

When you begin to pack and store things away its easier to move forward. The mere act of putting something into a box. It may be something you'll never need, something you are afraid of throwing away that you still feel the need to hold on to. You seal it all into a box for good and by placing it in its very own space, creates a sense of comfort, it gives you the "okay" to move forward. Once the box is sealed, and in position, you dust the palms of your hands off against each other, and for a moment you think you are ready to finally move on.

I hide and stack my boxes like Tetris pieces in my dark closet. The closed up and forgotten room becomes more and more crammed as the days, the months and the years flow by. The room itself needs a box I could place it into and just forget about it.

Then comes days like today when I dare to open the door. I gently pull out each box and set them out on the floor in front of me. I glide my hands across their tops and let my palms lie flat upon the larger ones beckoning the salty tears to descend, down my cheeks like falling dewdrops on a morning lily's flower petal.

My heart races at speeds not humanly possible. Perhaps the reason for it sounding as if though it's beating against my chest is because I have placed my very heart and everything it feels and desires into a box and have sealed it up tightly. Before removing any other box, I'll need to remove the tape off of the box of my heart.

I can no longer resist the urge to remove the seal from the oldest and most tattered box. The box that started this unusual strange and unconventional collection. The box that towers the rest in size. This container is sealed with both silver duct tape and wrapped up tightly with twine.

I pull a knife out from under my foot to cut the seals. I break each layer of twine and tape with the sharp blade. The binds proceed to snap loudly against the carton as the resistance is no longer a factor and the purpose of restraint is no more. The box and all it holds is free.

*** Box #1 ***

I slowly lift the lid and peer inside... immediately I see his face and like flashes of lightning during an electrical storm, visions of it all swarms past me. The force pushes me back a bit, taking my balance away from me but only for a second, yet my strength moves me forward and holds me upright. So much commotion over one single box... but it was everything... it was him... his role... his significance... he was my father.

My chest tightens, and my eyes grow large swelling up with tears. Uncontrollable anger fills every inch of my being as my previous disposition of subtle indifference fades and sinks deep beneath the floorboards.

They say time heals all wounds, but there are somethings that will always remain broken and belong stashed up in boxes. There are somethings that just don't belong and should have no place in this dream called life. I have always believed things happen for a reason, but for this... I don't ever think I'll discover that said reason.

Evil can sprout up and grow in the most unpredictable and unusual places. It can take over someone's soul and make them behave like a monster and rip apart everyone and everything you've ever known. And life as you know it can be turned upside down losing its sense and value.

For every girl, there is one man who is responsible for setting the tone for her life. This man is her father. By definition, he is the man who gives care and protection. For me as a child, my father was my hero. He was unbelievably understanding, level headed and lived a life of integrity.

I looked up to him and aspired to be just like him. He was the main pillar for our family, even among his friends, co-workers, acquaintances and our community. I idolized him... I admired his diligent work ethic and desired a career for myself where I would also have the opportunity to positively impact the lives of others within my industry and my community.

I craved the type of importance that he had seemingly constructed. I wanted to be wherever he was. I'd beg for him to let me tag along...

At his office, I'd sit at his desk and illustrate drawings on his legal pads. Imagining I was busy completing an important assignment, I was just like him. I worked diligently on my drawings knowing they were helping him get his job done, we were a team. My father held an important title within his industry. His role required him to find job assignments for construction laborers so they could in return support their families. I watched countless people come in and ask for his help. He worked tirelessly making as many calls and sending out as many emails as it would take to find them work. He never gave up; he understood the meaning of being the provider, the man.

The father.

My father wasn't just handed his position and title; he earned it. Like myself, he never finished college and relied on his tenacious work ethic and brilliant mind to create a career to support his family. He started working as a laborer right out of high school and migrated through the different trades educating himself on the construction industry.

He quickly grasped the concept of the relationship between politics and construction and jumped at the opportunity to advance as a business leader. In order to obtain his desired role he had to be voted in... and every election, he received almost every single vote in his favor. He served on different boards across the community and started supporting local politicians to secure the future of his trade. He'd allow me to tag along and attend board meetings for the city, and offer up my ideas on strategies to clean up the community.

I accompanied him to fancy political fundraisers. I'd dress myself up in fancy ball gowns and travel to the finest and most exclusive spots throughout the city. I was awarded the luxury of meeting Senators, State Representatives, Governors and Mayors across the state and across the country. They all knew my dad and would rave about how amazing he was. In those moments I was so proud to be his daughter. Because of my adoration for my father, I wished to impress him.
I studied vigorously at school and took on more responsibility around the house.

When my father stared down at me, and gave me his attention from the corner of my eye, I could see the smile lingering on his face and this I craved.

As time went by and as I aged from an adolescent into a teenager, he seemed to change. His hours at work and business trips away grew longer. His marriage became a struggle and I noticed a deep change in his eyes. He lost his luminosity. He wasn't filled with light anymore, and he seemed to be worn out and defeated all the time. His soul was stolen from him. I felt rejected. I felt like whatever I did; it was never good enough. My confidence in myself started to fade.

The depression sinking into every part of his existence, every vein in his body had been overtaken. There were days where he'd want to sleep all the time and had little interest in anything anymore. With his new lack of energy and interest, we grew apart. It was as if he didn't care for me at all, and I started doubting myself, and my confidence began to weaken.

Around this same time frame, my grandfather's health started diminishing. This created a very sore subject because he wasn't very close with his parents. I on the other hand absolutely adored them. My grandmother was my "go to" person.

I looked up to her and seek out her advice on life. We'd spend hours chatting on the phone and exchanged letters due to our significant physical distance apart.

Early one morning before the sun had a chance to peak over the fields we received a call. It was my grandmother on the other end of the phone informing us that my grandfather had experienced a stroke and was being admitted to the hospital. I stood alone in the downstairs living room with my father overcome with emotions of fear and grief. Everyone else in our home was asleep. But me? I was right there for him. Prepared to support the father I dearly loved.

My father hung up the phone after ending his conversation with my grandmother and just started sobbing. I had never seen him like this before. He hugged me tightly, and I stood still trying to console him, trying to be every support that he had ever been for me.

At some point however, I began to feel uncomfortable. The embrace was awkward and seemed as if it wouldn't end. I nonchalantly pulled away and tried to encourage him to get some rest. He proceeded forward and kissed me. This was not a kiss a father gives his daughter, and I immediately felt my stomach drop as his lips touched mine. His mouth was open. I immediately jerked away. Feeling ashamed and embarrassed, I attempted to fathom up any idea I could imagine to excuse his inappropriate behavior.

Maybe he was still somewhat in a sleep like stage... or just very upset from the news and wasn't sure what he was doing. Confused and ashamed at the same time I tried to make sense of it by getting some rest myself.

It was difficult to sleep after that. I was hopeful he would forget about it and I would too. Then came other similar occasions where he would become inappropriate with me. I remember I'd be sleeping or trying to take a nap and he'd lay down next to me and embrace me. The man I once looked up to, no longer saw his daughter. Blinded by dark lusts of his mind. I could feel him up against me. Again, embarrassed and ashamed I'd get up.

I would tell him I wasn't tired or needed to get homework done to avoid any further embarrassing conversation.

My father never forced himself onto me so I was very confused about what was going on and how I should feel or respond to it. I kept telling myself that maybe I was wrong. Maybe I felt uncomfortable because I was not familiar with this sort of affection. Eventually, I had enough. I gathered up the courage to tell an adult what was happening.

My step mother and I during that time hadn't been getting along. She was going to school and was absent from home a lot due to her class load. I felt like a lot of the household responsibilities were falling on my shoulders.
I spent a lot of my time watching over my younger siblings and at times felt as if I was taken for granted. Regardless of our current relationship, I believed I could trust her and could no longer hold onto my dark secret that was slowly digging away at me.

Eating on any bits of sanity I still had left.

On a summer afternoon, I found her folding laundry in our dining room. I stood next to her and picked up a towel casually to help. I refolded the same towel over and over again and while I forced my mouth to work. Finally, the words came out. I muttered that there was something I needed to talk to her about but wasn't sure how to even begin. She reassured me that anything I would tell her would stay between her and I. So, at that moment I just threw up the inevitable word vomit. I told her about the different incidents with my father.

I described how he'd lay next to me and push himself against me, how he kissed me that morning with his mouth open, and just how awful, disgusting and wrong everything felt.

She immediately stopped folding and turned toward me, and her face was filled with shock and sadness. As I had done previously, I saw her mind race as she searched it rigorously for excuses for him. She said that my dad was going through a lot of stress. Work was becoming more of a burden, and my grandfather's fading health was taking a toll on him. She reminded me that he was a good man and he'd never do anything to hurt me, that he loved me.

She expressed how he'd be absolutely devastated if he knew I felt this way about him. She explained that he wasn't one to physically show affection, so maybe that was why I felt so uncomfortable.

I immediately sunk to the floor in shame. She was his wife, so I knew she had to be right. He was my father, why would a father purposely be inappropriate with his daughter.

I never told anyone else about it again. After that conversation, I avoided being alone with him and all physical contact. I drew away more from my family. I spent as much time as I could with my high school boyfriend. As soon as I graduated high school, I moved out.

My dad eventually got divorced and separated from his wife and remarried. I had also married my high school sweetheart, and we purchased a home together. I saw my family rarely, so my desire to have a family of my own was growing. I wasn't very happy in my marriage but kept trying to get pregnant. I felt having a child would fulfil my life and bring joy into our marriage. I wasn't able to conceive, and I watched my relationship crumble right before my eyes.

My husband was a very possessive man and didn't want me to associate myself with anyone. We started working opposite shifts for work, and I spent all my free time alone. I created an isolated life for myself without even realizing it by submission unto him. Isolation became so normal, it was if I knew no other way, or had no other choice. He didn't understand and didn't even try.

He was a very selfish person. He was very controlling and mentally abusive. He isolated me as much as possible in fear I would leave him for someone else.

On a random afternoon, I got a call from my sister. She warned me that she had something really important to say and wanted to come by my house that evening to talk to me in person. I was nervous. I thought maybe she was going to say she was pregnant.

So being the daydreamer I am, getting ahead of myself I played that scenario out in my head. I wanted to be a mother so bad and hadn't had any luck at it yet. I became excited at the thought of being an Aunt. I started imagining up plans in my mind. We had an extra bedroom she could move into if she needed somewhere to go. I could help her, and everything would be perfect.

Just perfect.

My sister finally arrived, and at this point, I'm pretty excited for the news. She has an upset look on her face, but since she was still a teenager, I assumed that was normal. She sat down with me on my living room sofa and told me that what she was about to say was hard, but she had a feeling I would understand.

Then she told me.

My heart stopped immediately. Tears came flooding down my cheeks, and I threw my arms around her and apologized. Everything he did to me, his hands on my body. I saw it and imagined my little sister instead of myself under those incestuous hands. Touched by the man we esteemed and once loved.

He had been touching her. He would touch them in their privates and penetrate them with his fingers. My father was the monster under our beds, keeping us from the sweet dreams everyone wishes upon us before we head off to bed. He was the nightmare we struggled to wake up from.

Everything I felt about my father was real. He knew what he was doing, and not only was he doing it to me, he was taking it further and molesting my little sister.

Every negative emotion you can imagine ran through my entire body. I was furious. The things she told me he did to her made my blood boil.

Immediately I wanted to hunt him down and cause unspeakable pain upon him. Instead like a heatwave hitting, feelings of guilt ran across my being.

Why didn't I trust myself?
Why didn't I tell someone else about it?
Why didn't I think it could be happening to one of my sisters as well?

Could I have possibly saved her from all of this?
I answered my questions with tears of regret and just hugged my sister and promised her he would pay for all the horrendous things he did.

Within that same week, the investigation had begun. What added another unpleasant element to the situation was the fact that I was an employee at the local county emergency dispatch center and knew everyone working on his case.

I had been there for about a year and a half, so I had developed great working relationships with the personnel in the most of the Sheriff's departments. When the investigator's questions it was humiliating, to say the least. I didn't want anyone to know these intimate details of what I now called my life, especially people I had to interact with daily. I didn't want people to uncover my shame and to judge me for being related to an absolute monster or to pity me. They tried to comfort me by telling me everything would be okay, and they would make sure justice would be served.

During the investigation, I was told to act completely normal as if I knew nothing. I was encouraged to continue talking with my dad as if nothing had happened. This was extremely difficult.

The mere thought of my father made me want to go out on a violent savage rampage, returning to my sister with his scalp as a trophy of our defeat over him. With these types of dark and vivid thoughts running through my mind, I knew acting *normal* would be agonizing and almost impossible.

One night while I was busy at work I got a call from my sister. She was crying and asked me to come over. She said she was scared and that her mom was really upset and she didn't know what to do. I threw off my headset that was attached to the 911 phone system, ripping it right out from its outlet. In a panic, I carelessly abandoned my post and left my station. I hopped into my car and sped to their house unaware of any other vehicle on the roadway.

I get there in what seemed like a flash. I throw open the door and see my family gathered in the living room. Everyone was in a heightened emotional state with red eyes full of tears. My sister's mom tells me that my other little sister, the baby of the family, just told her that my dad had molested her as well. At that moment, my eyes turned red and dark like theirs, and my body went numb.

I spoke with my littlest sister, only seven years old mind you, and she laid out everything that had happened to her. I was shocked and completely appalled that someone could ever do the awful things she described to me and even more alarmed by how a father could ever touch his daughter that way.

I wanted him dead.

I wanted it more than I had ever wanted anything in my life. At that very moment, if someone had handed me a gun and told me where he was, there is no doubt in my mind that he would have been buried six feet under after greeting me.

***

The last time I saw my father was the day after Christmas. I sat across from him at the dinner table. Their home was beautifully displayed with lavish winter decorations and a generous holiday feast was prepared and presented in front of us. I couldn't manage to even look at his face while I sat in hidden disgust and anger. I do however clearly remember looking over at my sisters and telling them with my mind; *we're almost done.* I'll take care of it. I'm going to make this right.

***

The day the detectives were finally prepared to question my father I received a call from him. He told me that the police were looking for him and asked if I knew why. I lied and said I had no idea, but I was good friends with most of the cops so not to worry, that he'd be fine. Finally, the police went and picked him up. Of course, that would be the day I was on the schedule to work. I felt so uneasy knowing he was right down the hall from me in a tiny interrogation room with my coworkers. The hours seemed to pass by so slowly while they questioned him. Finally, they released him from the room and the station. They pulled me aside in confidence and told me it went well. They said that he didn't confess to all of it, but enough of it to have him charged. I felt a bit of relief but knew it wasn't over yet. I knew he was free and now he knew that we all came forward against him.

If I wasn't a mess before, I sure was now. I told my husband I was deathly afraid. What if he wanted to kill us for telling? He was going to lose everything, his family, his job, his good name. Everything he was, he wasn't anymore.

My husband could not understand how I felt and didn't even try to relate to me.

I couldn't sleep at night and didn't want to be touched. The furthest thing from my mind was sex, for more than apparent reasons. He became resentful and even more emotionally abusive accusing me of sleeping with other men. I decided I couldn't be married to him any longer. I couldn't endure any more pain and games of the mind. It was clear that our marriage just wasn't working and I had lost all interest in my husband and trying to make it work. I didn't care anymore.

***

My patience for the justice system was growing thin. The investigation was dragging. I spoke to the detectives daily asking why charges hadn't been pressed against him. Their answer was that the judge wanted more evidence. They asked me to have a recorded phone conversation with him to see if I could get him to confess to more, so I obliged. It was gut-wrenchingly awful. I sat in a cold white room with three men and had the most uncomfortable phone conversation of my life. The lies that came across the phone lines from my dad's lips into my ears were distressing.

My father kept telling me he couldn't remember anything and that my sister and her mom wanted to crucify him and ruin his life.

The phone call was ultimately a fail and just another pointless, painful memory to add to the box.

***

I remember the day his warrant for arrest was issued. A woman I worked with brought the file to me. I held it in my hands and blankly starred at it while my mind raced in circles. I sobbed a bit and knew this was a beginning to an end. I watched as she entered it into the computer system and then we waited.

Finally, an officer from our Sheriff's Department signalled our center by toning up and then spoke to us across the police district radio. The police beat assigned to the area of his residence called it in. They had him in custody. They were bringing him to the jail in the back of a squad car. He was going to be right below me in the basement jail. His wrists would be tightly secured in handcuffs while they inked his fingers for prints to be properly processed and booked. They would direct him to a corridor and then placed in a cell behind bars.

In the dispatch area where I worked there were tiny televisions posted near the corners of the ceiling that would show the security footage of the jail. I watched as the sally port doors opened and the police car with him inside pulled in. I watched him get brought in. Hands behind his back in cuffs he was processed just as I had imagined numerous times in my dreams.

I felt numb again. The voices around me were like that of ghosts, just faint noises all blended in harmony. My phone started to vibrate, and when I looked down at my caller identification on my phone's screen, I was surprised.

He was calling me from downstairs in the jail. I quietly walked away from my desk and took the call alone in the hallway. I recall the smell of that hallway, burnt popcorn and stale old coffee. I paced back up and down the hall as he spoke and I gathered all my strength not to break down and cry.

He told me that my sister and her mom told awful lies about him. He said that he would be going to prison and he needed me to do him a favor and became silent. My mind began to race... Is he going to apologize? Maybe he is going to confess and wants me to look after my siblings... then he spoke...

"Ev, I need you to help me with my finances while I'm away. My wife will probably leave me and you are the only one who can do it. I trust only you. Make sure I have money on my books for commissary..."

I took a huge step forward and bent over. I pushed my ear closer into the phone as if I misheard what he had just plainly said to me. I was FURIOUS. He didn't know it, but this would be the last time we'd ever speak to each other. These would be his last words to me. And out of all the things, he could possibly say to clear his conscious he had the audacity to ask me to take care of him. I boldly and simply replied "sure." And that was it.

In a few days, his bond was reduced and he was back out free to roam. That's when I decided to take a closer look at the court paperwork. I had a suspicion there were political ties to the judge. I made a call to his company's office. My dad's partner at the office was aware of the situation and supported my sisters and I.

I asked his partner to check their accounts payable log and to see if they had made any campaign contributions to his current case's judge.

Sure, enough there it was in black and white. I began to realize that the length of the process was due to this, and the reduced bail was the same. I was so angry and distraught that a judge was bought in a criminal sex case involving minors.

Immediately a copy of the campaign donation was sent to the State's Attorney's office and they asked that a new judge be assigned to the case. As time crept by, I grew into a depression. I didn't care much for anything anymore, and my faith in the judicial system and in God even was fading.

I didn't want to go to work anymore because I was embarrassed and ashamed by my father. I wanted to go out and drink it all away to forget.
My urge to runaway grew, and I decided to leave the country, so I enlisted into the US Air Force and quit my job at the dispatch center. Because of my dad's case and my pending divorce, the dates for my departure for basic training kept being extended out after an official assignment.
After about three different date changes they told me it'd be best to take an honorable discharge and re-enlist once everything was settled, but I never went back.

I started working odd jobs and partying my ass off to numb the pain since there seemed to be no other escape.

***

A year or so down the road my dad was finally sentenced. He managed to drag out the court process for an entire year before taking a plea bargain. He was finally charged with 22 counts of felony aggravated criminal sexual abuse to a child/family member. He was sent to prison on 2/26/2009 and is not set for release until 2/5/2018.

****

My floor is now flooded with tears and memories. My hands reach out to gather them up as quickly as possible and stuff them back in their box. I know the sides of the box are stretched and slightly broken. I understand that I will have to re-open it again soon. But still, I push its fitted top back on tightly. I grab the ball of twine, and rapidly I wrap it around the box, causing cuts and slivers on the palms of my hands from the rapid movements. I secure the box even more with duct tape. The noise of each pull of stretched out tape somehow calms my soul.

I place it in my arms and stand to my feet all in one motion. I move forward to the closet and stand on the tips of my toes. I elevate the box with my fingertips to place it on the very top shelf. I barely slide it on the shelf's surface. I make one quick jump into the air to hit the box's side pushing it to the farthest point back on the shelf... This box will always be the hardest to reach, most difficult to open and will always be almost impossible to store away...

Evalee Renae Torres

Flowers On An Open Grave

I lay flowers at the foot of my grave to signify the death of my past. While I rejoice in the birth of a new being, a new spirit, a new life.
Melody Wilson

Sitting in my room catching myself thinking about all the things done to me, all the things that were said. I realized that I had just gone to The Apollo with my daughter and auditioned, I was good. I was good and they turned me down. Now let's see, how many times and ways I second guess myself before I completely sink myself into a depressed oblivion?

I gotta keep my composure. Auri was standing there looking at me with those huge gorgeous eyes.

"Mommy, what happened?" My motherly instinct tugging at my heart, telling me that I needed to reassure I was ok.

"You made it Auri."

Auri looked at me with fear and concern. "Well, what about you mommy?" That in itself tore me up. I looked up at her.

"No baby, I didn't make it."

The disbelief brought tears to her eyes, "But why mommy? You were good."

Here I go. Unable to cry or to get upset.

I couldn't show what was in my head and my heart this time because I had to be strong for my daughter, not knowing that I would be blessed enough to be brave for another child who also didn't make it. For the entire drive home, I'd sit smiling with an aching heart. Something that I learned to do so many years ago, and I fought back the tears. My heart ached and I fought back the tears.

Angry and beating myself up I pondered. What did I do? Was I not good enough? Am I good enough? I might as well forget about this. Who was I fooling? I'm too old for this shit.

Again, beating myself up and blaming myself. And then out of nowhere for the first time, it happened.

Daddy. I lost my voice that day you know. I was silenced. I used to sing, dance, write. There was nothing I couldn't do. Daddy silenced me. Daddy took my voice.

...

I missed out on a lot of years of opportunities because I have remained that thirteen-year-old all my life. In October 2006, I grew a little older, and as we speak, I am getting even older. And before we know it, I'll catch up to my 33.

I have been going to incest survivor meetings now since October. A lot has happened for me and a lot of things have changed. I have opened old wounds and exposed myself to all kinds of vulnerability. Vulnerability to my past, to those old wounds, my pain, and scorned heart. Everything makes sense to me now. God has blessed me with sight, clear sight, and sensibility. I am asking that you do not rush through this, it is just a beginning for me in my healing process. But it is only the first step in me finding my voice, exploring my writing and my story has to be told.

I will not protect my father anymore.

My willingness to heal will open wounds for all of us, but for that, I cannot sympathize. I do hope that it will bring about positive change and mutual respect as we all continue to live, love and grow. Me sharing my open wounds is my way of getting my voice back.

Where My Story Begins.

It is the fall of 1986.   It wasn't a long day today.
It was a Sunday, and I had already been to
church with my dad as usual.   Today I was cute.
I had on my favorite blue tiger striped dress with
the ruffles around the hips, black stockings and
black pumps.   I was just starting to fill out up top
and my waist was mad thin, and at the age of
thirteen, I began to acknowledge when I looked
cute.

Church was church as normal. Reverend
McDowell delivered a beautiful and moving
sermon, and Deacon Jones made sure to do his
routine 'Sunday Shout' dance five minutes
before the sermon ended. Thank God he didn't
hurt anybody. Last time he knocked off Sister
Louise's wig, I thought it was hilarious, but I'm
certain she was mortified.
It was one of those days after church when I was
done cooking dinner, cleaning the kitchen and I
could relax because my dad whom I have been
living with for a while, had decided to hang out
for the day. This left me with the house to
myself. I used to love having the house to
myself.

The first thing that I would do was crank up my favorite albums on the record player, blast them as loud as I could and run through the house singing and dancing, putting on my very own concert. Singing to the top of my lungs *Shannon's* "Let the Music Play" and then topping it off with my *Jennifer Holiday's* show stopper, *I am Love.* But I was missing my background dancers and singers. My sisters and little brother.

It was my weekend. No visitation. No babysitting. After my chores and outstanding performance. I settled in on the couch, still in my blue tiger striped dress with stockings, and watched an episode of *Rags to Riches.* Always noticing when there was only one black character, this time *Tisha Campbell.*
Boy has that girl come a long way, going on to do *Martin* and *My Wife and Kids.* It was bearable only because of the dancing and singing. Outside of that, it wasn't much to watch. That's just my opinion.

Well, it wasn't my intention to spend the rest of the evening on the couch, but an unexpected visitor made me change my mind.

I am terribly afraid of rodents, and there was one in particular who decided to stop by this very night.

I wasn't exactly sure where *Murray* came from, but he was not welcome to stay. Murray was a little gray mouse that at every given chance, would peep at me from behind the large floor model television that sat in the middle of my father's living room floor. And me being the scaredy cat that I am, I decisively refused to move until he decided to leave or until my father got home and made him leave.

So of course, with me being afraid to get off the couch, I sat there most of the evening watching television. After *Rags to Riches* ended, The *Stepford Children* came on. And boy was I glad that there was something interesting for me to watch. Because again, I wasn't moving from that spot.

I sat there scared out of my wits, watching TV and more so watching the corner of the TV looking for Murray until my father came in. I could always look at my dad and tell when he had been hanging out with his cousin Donald or our other cousins who always liked to have a good time socializing.

He came in and went straight for the love seat that sat next to the couch. He laid back with his brown leather jacket still on, closed his eyes, put his hand around my neck and shoulder as I was lying with my back to him on the couch and said "Daddy is a little high tonight baby." Well, I was thirteen, I knew what a little high meant. It meant that he and his cousins were smoking those joints again. Weed was no secret to me and my brothers and sisters, my father had introduced it to us when I was about five years old. It wasn't bad.

I sat there on the couch watching *The Stepford Children* trying to explain to my dad what the show was about while he drifted in and out of his highness. It didn't matter that I was sitting there scared as hell, worried if Murray was going to come from behind the television and attack me. My dad was so out of it that eventually he passed out and went to sleep.

Or so I thought.

I sat there watching TV, finally content as there was no sign of Murray. Hell, maybe he went home. I leaned down on the couch trying to relax until I felt my father's hand slowly slide down the front of my dress. He was sleeping, so I figured it was a natural reaction. To be on the safe side and because his hand was so close to my BREAST, I figured it was better for me to slide down so that he wasn't touching them.

But now I'm thinking, "What the hell?" Because instead of his hand resting where it fell, it continued to move as I continued to move until I almost slid off the damn couch.

Well to avoid sitting on the floor in my blue tiger striped dress where Murray could finally boldly attack me right there in the middle of the floor, I sat up in the middle of the couch. It was hard to figure out what had just happened or what could have been going on. I looked over at my father and he was sleeping. Because he didn't move or make a sound, I figured maybe it was just me. But because I was still confused about it and just wasn't sure, I couldn't move from that spot. So, I sat there and tried to figure it out until *The Stepford Children* went off and I realized the credits were rolling on the television screen. To this day, I still couldn't tell you what happened at the end of that show.

Once I was able to snatch myself back to reality, I got up and went to my bedroom so that I could get ready for school the next morning.

I took my shower as usual and then put on my nightgown. It was nothing special, just a regular old grandma gown. You know the kind with ruffles around the neck in the front of the gown that buttoned up in the front with ruffles around the wrist. I was dressed and ready for bed when my dad called me into the living room.

I kept thinking about what happened earlier, positive that it was all in my head. And most importantly, I was thinking we didn't play with my dad like that. When he said *jump*, we broke our necks to ask, *how high?*

I went into the living room to see what he wanted. He asked me if I would sit down and braid his hair. There was nothing unusual about this because I had done his hair plenty of times. My father had long shoulder length hair and it was 1986 so he was rocking the what? The Jeri Curl!

My father was an attractive man. Tall with broad shoulders and very muscular. He was a karate instructor in the art of Tae Kwon Do. He also worked with the EMS. He had women galore. Everybody loved my father; he was the people's person and what I call a *local celebrity*. He sat down on the floor between my legs while I sat on the couch.

I began to comb his hair and then began to braid it. As I braided the third or fourth braid, whichever was closest to me finishing, it happened.

My father took his hand and began to rub my thigh. Just as I had done earlier when he had fallen asleep in the love seat, I moved my thigh hoping that he would not do it again and continued to braid his hair like nothing had happened. But then he did it again. This time I didn't hesitate. I got up and went straight to my room without saying a word. I was nervous, but I thought I was safe. And eventually, I fell asleep.

I don't remember what time it was, but it was very late in the night or early in the morning rather when I woke out of my sleep. It wasn't clear as to what was going on. I woke up to someone touching me between my legs. I had never been touched by anyone before, well except an experience that I had with another little girl my age, but that's another story. When I woke up and realized that I was being touched, I couldn't understand what was going on.

I was thinking *I know this ain't my uncle touching me.*

My father's brother also lived with us. After that, it was evident that it wasn't my uncle on top of me because when he was touching me, he was moaning and in the midst of his moans he called me Linda. Linda was my brother's mother.

My father's girlfriend or ex-girlfriend, whatever they were doing at the time.

He continued to touch me, moaning and groaning, and I didn't know what in the world to do. I remained still. Immobile. He touched me, my father sucked my breasts, and before the sun came up, he put on a condom, he spread my legs apart, he climbed on top of me, inserted himself inside of me and proceeded to take my virginity.

OH, MY GOD!!!!!!!!!!!!!!
My head screamed while he was on top of me, riding me. If you could hear the screams coming from my wide eyes in the dark, I would have woken all the neighbors.

But nobody heard my screams.
Nobody came to my rescue.

I just had to lie there and feel him go up and down on me, inside me, hurting me. More and more tears began to fall each time he would jerk up and down on my thirteen-year-old body built with a sixteen-year-old frame. I had nothing inside me that would allow me to open my mouth, to push him away. His Jeri curl head fixed into my shoulder.

To this day, I'll never forget how that sticky mess feels against my skin. I stayed there, letting him, allowing him, not stopping him from stroking away twenty years of my life. Not knowing that at that moment he was stripping away all that was good in me. That was the night; I lost my spirit. That was the night I lost my will.

With my eyes, wide open unable to fall asleep. I lay there wet, not sure with what and too scared to move. The night had no end and sleep would not overtake my body. The next morning I was afraid of what I was going to see when I got up because now I was all sticky. I grabbed my things and went for my shower. Assuming that if my father wasn't going to say anything, I wasn't going to say anything. Besides what the hell was I gonna say?

On my way out of my room, my dad called my name. He startled me sitting in the living room fully dressed at 6:30 am. Slumped back in another small chair that sat at the other end of the couch, with his hand over his face. He called me over to him and he hugged my neck crying, apologizing, saying how sorry he was, and that it was never going to happen again. I believed him too.

It was all a lie; my father would continue to violate me, over and over and over and over and over, and over.

Letter to my family.

To my mother whom I love very much. I do not hold any resentment towards you for the pain, the mental anguish, the confusion that my father, your husband inflicted upon me. Since my recovery, I have learned that a lot of your actions and your behaviors are and have was based on those things of which you experienced growing up, and for that, I empathize. Through our culture, we have been taught that as long as we have God and the church, we don't need anything and anyone else, but through trial and error, I have learned that that is not true. God created certain people and resources for a reason. And my reason for verbalizing this to you is because although you feel that you have overcome all obstacles associated with your past through your spirituality, your thoughts and opinions, how you choose to deal with me regarding this matter, lets me further know, that you may need to seek counseling to resolve certain issues. If you choose not to do this for myself and my sisters, then you may want to do it for yourself. Fruitful and healthier relationships occur out of it, along with a sense of self, strength and well-being.

Understanding your fears, hesitations, and insecurities, helps you to overcome them. And like you, for so many years it started to feel like I was completely losing whatever voice my father, had not taken from me. Again, I do not hold resentment towards you for the past. However, I'm holding resentment right now because I haven't received the critical support that I feel like I need most of all from you.

I will continue to say and let it be known until it is understood, that I ALLOWED myself to deal with my father all of these years since he raped and molested me because my mother and my sisters chose to deal with him. When he got locked up, I didn't want to visit him, but I did because you did, all of you did. I never wanted to make gifts for him. But I did because all of you did. I never wanted to see him whenever he came over to see you guys after he got out. But nobody cared.
Who knew my cries inside my head when he would be there? How you had the nerve to say "You can't let your father..."
When I was at that vulnerable age, there was no voice in me that was strong enough to ask for your help or even to express how much seeing him was killing me inside.

At the age of 33, I stand before the people whom I think love me the most and I beg and plead for your help. Well, today ma, I can't let you say these words to me. When your husband satisfied his inhumane and barbaric cravings on occasion or whenever he felt like it, I came to you. I was in pain, and I said to you, "Ma, I wanna come home." And you told me no. You told me that I wanted to be grown and that's what I asked for and each time you made me go back to that man to that place, to that hell, that darkness. You never asked me why, you never asked me why I had dark circles around my eyes or why I was so pale, or why my clothes were falling off from the weight I was losing.

My coach and gym teacher did because he was the only one who saw what you, my mother failed to see. I relive that same pain every single time I lose or misplace something. A jacket, a keychain.

I left my little blue jean jacket in a friend's car. Assured that I'd get it back in a day or so, I still panicked. I wanted to drive over an hour to retrieve my jacket because that's how lost I was. Because of what he did I have terrible attachment issues to things and losing them causes me severe panic.

Sitting in the parking lot, crying like a baby, bewildered and not knowing what to do over a freaking jacket.
Who held my hand? Who cursed them out for burning my possessions for the bull that they drummed up in their heads? Why did you never support me?

I was a child who was steady having my heart ripped apart by the people I love, and because of that, I experience mounds and mounds of painful emotions every day from various things.

The night I stopped by your job, you told me that I was blaming you. You went on to say that it wasn't your fault. I was thirteen years old. Whose fault was it? Was it mine? You didn't send me to my father, your husband to have him rape, molest, and have sex with me. But you wouldn't let me come home when I asked. It took me to get sick and fall down on my hands and knees crying like you said I would, for me to be allowed to come back to your home. Then and only then.

Whose fault was it? Was it mine?

This pattern has gone on long enough. You were molested by the men in your family, and nobody stood up and protected you. And then you grew up around them because nobody told you that it wasn't ok. You grew up, and your husband did what he did to me. You kept going with that curse. The tradition. You made it ok for us to associate ourselves with a pedophile. Would you have done that if it was some man in the streets? If some man in the streets had raped and molested one of your children, would you still have let us talk to him? What is the difference, because he was your husband because they were your family?

And the curse stops here with my children and me. As long as you guys continue to deal with this man in this capacity, and the support for me and my children is not there, we will not associate ourselves with anything that has to do with down south which includes you.

To my sister TA. It has been selfish on everyone's part to not yet have acknowledged the amount of pain you have been experiencing. The night when you helped me pack my things to leave our father's home, you found my letter.

You found the words that I wrote describing the pain, the torment, the torture. You read about the rotten, befouled things that our father did to me, to my body. Staying up crying all night. I remember waking up to go to school the next morning, and you were still crying. Had it not been for your courage to give that letter to someone, (which is what you always have been the biggest tattle tale, no one would have known my pain. And for you I am grateful. We have not always seen eye to eye in our lives. I realize now that a lot of the things that you said to me were out of anger, hurt, and frustration. You too are a victim. But I have always admired your courage to speak up. I hope that at some point when you are done reading, you will have conquered a piece of YOUR voice that you lost a long time ago when my innocence and your voice was stolen.

And you will be able to speak up about things that you have been holding in for so long that have almost deadened and hardened your soul.

I don't remember verbatim what you read that day; I only know that if it was as vivid as Auri tends to write now, then I know I was very detailed.

I only remember what I had to read in court. But I do want you to know that for once, your pain is recognized.

We were born into some curse or whatever label you want to put on it, but it can only be broken once we stand up for it and against it. One thing that mamma has always said to us and I know to be true is that our children is our key to life, to love, and to happiness. We can't take care of them without taking care of ourselves. For us to continue to grow and prosper, we have to nurture them, their beings.

We can't get so wrapped up in our everyday lives and the people that we CHOOSE to deal with and lose sight of what GOD HAS GIVEN US. Our children did not ask to be brought into this world, so, therefore, it is our responsibility to make sure that they are taken care of to the best of our ability.

I firmly stand by what I feel in that God blesses us with life for a purpose. At some point, you gotta wonder, what is your purpose? And these sorry ass people that we bring into our lives have no idea and definitely can't offer or even decipher our purpose. Because of our sickness, we have allowed very unhealthy people to encompass our lives.

If you take the first step, God will do the rest. I'm the spokesperson for God is capable of all things. Know that with all that is in me, I love you.

I know that we have hurt each other with words in the past, but that's what we knew. We now know that there's another way. There is always another way

I don't know or understand the violence that may come and go throughout the daily within your relationship, but what I will tell you is that it is detrimental to you and your children. Your oldest is going to be a modern "me" and if somebody doesn't grab hold to her soon, you're going to lose her. And I'm not saying lose her to the streets. Your kids love you. They have expressed that they're not happy. Not because of you, but because of the company you keep. They want to be with their mother and I'm quite sure anybody that is going to be healthy for their mother. I've offered for them to come stay here, but those kids are scared to leave in fear of what may happen to their mother. And I'm sorry, kids should not have to live like that. They can't function and have everyday lives in school wondering what is to unfold when they come home or later that night. It's not healthy, it's not fair, and you will be punished. I swear, you'll never get it right. I know. I was there and I never got it right, until I was ready to start looking at my bullshit and ready to start making changes. Take those kids, hug them, love them, embrace them, and remember where they came from. You carried those seeds. Those are your babies from your womb. Don't let them stray from you. Because as much as I love you, and most of the time you seem to be on my wavelength, I can't let my children come there if the atmosphere is not safe and healthy for them. I do not know why you still allow yourself to deal with our father in any capacity like you do. Maybe yours is the same as mine, because mom did, I don't know.

To my little sister, TR. You by far have been the most disappointing to me recently. I say that because you are the one that I have spoken with for the past couple of months. You were the first one that I told I had started going to the incest survivor meetings. You were the one who was being there and being supportive. And I trusted you.

I should have known when I got down there, and I asked you not to tell our father that I was home, and you were against it, that there would be problems. You felt like you didn't want to be placed in the middle. You offered me a false sense of security, and then you let me down. You made me feel like I was standing inside of a gate and on the other side was a huge pit bull ready to attack, and when you felt like it, you opened the gate and let him in. And that hurt me. Because of you and our mother you allowed me to feel that panic, that fear.

And the whole time you mimicked your mother in saying. "You can't let daddy..."

I can't let you. I can't let you make it seem like it's ok for me or my children to be subjected to this man who abused, molested, and raped me. You were young when everything happened. That's not to say that you weren't affected by what our father did. I do know beyond a shadow of a doubt that all of us were in some shape or form affected by his sickness. But maybe it has not affected you to the point for you to try to understand my plight in asking you to support me in that I don't want anything to do with that man right now. It's not a joke, it's not a game, and I'm serious.

It doesn't mean that I want to pass him on your steps. And it sure as hell does not mean that I want to look up out the windshield of my car and see him walking towards me carrying my son and you not stop him or warn me. And then you come to me and tell me to calm down. Please understand that I wasn't upset. I was mad as hell, and when you touched me to rub my back, my skin was on fire. You and your mother are definitely one in the same.

I always thought of you as spoiled, selfish and self-centered but I thought all of that had changed. We all have our problems, demons, or whatever to deal with, but you are no better than TA or me. And I swear to God on everything I love including you, if you ever speak to me like that again I will never speak to you again. And God hear me speak. I mean it. I won't let any of you hurt me with your words again. With all of that being said, I am very proud of you and how you have carried yourself and taken care of your children. For that, you can only be commended.

And I am extremely proud of you for what you have achieved through your education. I know beyond a shadow of a doubt, that whatever field you choose, be it a Physician Assistant or an actual Physician that you will do well and will excel far beyond most expectations. You have, like me grown leaps and bounds, but you still got a lot more growing to do.

To my father, to my protector, to my best friend and my confidant, to my lover, to my nothing.

I have gone over and over in my head what I would say to you if the time would come that I would say anything to you at all. It has been over 20 years since you touched what was rightfully mine, stuck your fingers inside me, put a condom on and viciously raped me.

Sitting here writing this I have a vile taste in my mouth and if it weren't for the fact that I didn't want to damage a perfectly good wireless keyboard, I'd throw up. What do you think about every day in that how I exist? Do you ask yourself and oh my God, have you ever cared?

You ever wonder how I sleep at night? You ever think about me fuckin somebody else? When I walk by do you still look at my ass?

*Do you wanna touch it? Do you still wanna
touch me? Remember when you used to tap on
the bathroom door, and peek inside to see if I
needed you to come wash my back, do you still
wanna do that? Do you miss me cooking meals
for you, like wifey? Do you remember the time
when I came home from spending the summer
in Maryland and as soon as ma drove off you
closed the door and pulled me close to you and
tried to put your mouth on me to kiss me, do
you still wanna do that? Do you still feel like
explaining to me why you raping me made it
the best thing for me and you?*

*Did I feel like the grown up women?
Huh daddy?*

*Oh, my god.
What are you doing?
Please, daddy, don't touch me like that.
Daddy, no.
No. No. No.*

*What did you think when you heard me say
that? Or was it because I had let it happen so
many times that it didn't matter. I know you
didn't hear me the first time because the
screams were all in my head.*

But I know you heard me. I know you heard me when I asked you to stop. I know you heard me when I told you stop. I know you felt me when I fought you trying to get you stop. I was your daughter you sick son of a bitch.

I woke up one day and I let go of a dream. A dream that you took from me. I spent twenty years of my life dealing with bullshit that you created.

I had unhealthy relationships, friendships with boyfriends, girlfriends, friends, family. I dated everything short of a fuckin monkey trying to figure it all out. I couldn't get anything right in my life because of you, and I lived in a constant state of bewilderment, anxiety, fear, panic, desperation, depression, holding myself back from people, places, things, and opportunities.

You silenced me. You stole my voice. And it is disheartening as hell at the age of thirty-three to feel like I'll never get the chance to do something that I felt like I was born to do because my time has passed.

Lauren-J. Covito   239

*And to know that with everything that is in me
I'm going to be there for my daughter. Hoping
and praying that I won't grow old with some
sick resentment or jealousy towards her
because she can live the life I felt like I wasn't
able to live. The messed up thing about all of
this is that for all these years I thought I was ok.
And it is thanks to your nephew, my cousin
David that you were ever afforded the
opportunity that you were given. Another thing
I think is foul is that I allowed you a place in my
life, and with that, you still became the same
manipulating motha fucka you've always been.
From the time that you went down south with
me and used me then scared the shit outta me
while I was pregnant. To the time you didn't
ask if you could come over and spend the night
and brought your girlfriend without asking me
and slept in my family room.*

*It's never ending with you. Too many times in
my life I have sat back and felt sorry for you
after what you did to me. After what you took
from me. My life was never the same. My life
with you was a living hell, a nightmare. I have
had multiple sex partners. I have slept with
guys whose face I'll never remember and names
I'll never know.*

Each time closing my eyes somehow letting them stroke away the pain. I let man after man, after man, after man take from me because you had taken what I thought was precious. I felt that I had nothing left to offer anyone and I never felt like I was good enough. I simply felt soiled. I put myself in situations that were detrimental and dangerous for me and my children, searching for that love. Instead of getting myself and my life together, I continued to hurt myself and allow myself to be hurt everyday by so many people. You taught me how to let someone hurt me and accept that as their love for me. Cause you were my daddy, my protector, and you hurt me, but you loved me.

I have walked around for years, intimidated by people. Always thinking that everybody was better, and never being sure of myself.

Do you even know how many talents I have and the things that I am capable of? Outside of singing, do you know I write the songs I sing? Do you know I have written poems and short stories? I am so many things, so many different people, but I'm not half the woman I could be for fighting with my reality, which is you and what you did to me.

I used to get a vile taste in my mouth when every man that I dated eventually turned out to be you and their very touch would make my skin crawl like maggots eating away at flesh. How do you feel when you're in a relationship, is it hard for you? It has always been hard for me. I've allowed myself to be used and abused over and over and over again, because of you. Just like you used to do me, over and over and over again. Because of you, I've been on my back more times than I can remember. There were times I had to worry. Have you ever gone through that, constantly worried about having to take an HIV test?

Let me ask you a question, are you still getting high? I bet you are. You ever wonder why I still talk to you? Do you really care? Do you think I'm supposed to? Do you feel like I owe you something? How do you think I'm able to talk to you? Was that shit conscious? Come on now, do you ever think about that shit? Do you ever think about you doing shit like that would fuck me up for the rest of my life? Do you realize that almost the whole town of Fairmont turned against me because I "lied on my daddy?"

Do you know I got teased and called names and ostracized by your crazy ass family because I "lied on my daddy?" Do you know I lost out on two years of my cousin's life because I didn't want to deal with you? And who the fuck are you to disregard my fuckin feelings like it's ok you selfish son of a bitch. Do you think about that shit?

Listen, did you know that I was going through all that shit when you were locked up? You know everybody turning against me and shit? Daddy, did you know I was 13? Did you know that I was going to have to deal with that and all them people at thirteen. What in the world!?! Man what was on your mind?

I know I got a lot of questions. But these are my random thoughts sometimes. I'm trying to fix it so that I don't think about you at all anymore. I think. But you know what? I say all of this to say to you, I ain't mad. About a week ago, for the first time, I allowed myself to hate you. I allowed myself to feel the pain of hating you. And after feeling that type of anger, rage, pain so deep within your soul somewhere in there you find your strength and that's what's happened to me. I needed to let you know that I get angry still thinking about you daddy, I do.

And for a long time, I was still scared, up to Thanksgiving, which is why I didn't want to see or talk to you when I was down there. You know, you do that old manipulating thing, and you almost got me again. You almost had me feeling sorry for you. But I quickly shook that.

My healing process has begun, in which at some point, my life will be completely manageable, functioning, healthy, and prosperous. And although I will be living my life with my past, it will be in my past. And I will learn and know how to love healthy like. And I will be free from your chains that held me for so many years. You took my innocence from me so long ago daddy, but I won't let you win. I'm fighting, and I'm becoming stronger every day. You know better than anyone how strong willed and determined I am. I was your protégé.

I sure wish I could have gotten my black belt. You put a halt on a lot of things. You know I done tore up and tore down a lot of things in my house and hurt myself in the process fueled by so much anger, hurt, and pain caused by you. Sometimes the rage is so great; I can see nothing through the red in my eyes. A lot of times, that's when I want to go for blood. You've made me have suicidal thoughts.

How would you have felt if one day after you climbed off me, I sat up on the edge of the bed with my clothes half off, reached up under my pillow, pulled out the .22, put it to my temple and with a quick motion? GONE.

God made me dismiss that thought. How could you have the audacity to come down to my house when I was with my first girlfriend and say to me, I hope what I did to you didn't make you this way. How typical. Please know and understand that I knew as young as seven that I was attracted to women, or rather at the time, other little girls.

So, to you, I do not owe my sexuality. You took everything else; you don't get that too.

Today daddy, where everyone chose to say to me, "You can't let your father," I'm saying to you, I won't let you control me and my life. I will not let you manipulate me and my life. I won't let you silence me. I hope I have done what I came to do and that I have served my purpose. I have been told within the past month or so that I am a very good writer. I write in a way that I evoke feelings and emotions. Let me know if that was the case for you...

Melody.

Later in my life, God has blessed me with the gift of expressing myself not only through song but through words in writing. I hope that everything that I have said to each of you resonates and continues to resonate and evoke feelings in you. Until changes have been made, curses have been broken, children are being protected, children are being heard, until wounds are ready to be reopened and healed so that our lives can move on happy with time. Time does not stop because we can't get it right, neither does our time span here on this earth. For whatever breath that God continues to bless us with, be wise, and use it kindly. Recognize God for all this He is worth. He is omnipotent. He is an artist with a sense of humor. He is all things, and without Him, we would not exist and nothing would be possible. And that's all that matters. For whatever changes any of you are experiencing right now, I ask that God be with you, and that's all I can do. What kind of messages are we sending to our children? With my children, it stops here. I will not show that to them. That is mixed messages, and very unhealthy, and very likely what they will grow up doing if we don't stop it now. What kind of trust are we teaching them to have? It doesn't scare you to know that one day we may see who

our children gravitate to negative tendencies based on some unhealthy behaviours that we may pass on to them because they're inconceivable to us? All of them need to be talked to now. We need to stop dead in our tracks with these unhealthy behaviors before we ruin or kids, and that's my last plea. *Mom, I ain't mad at you. I just want you to recognize your part in this whole thing. I still love my family; you're my family so what else am I supposed to do. And contrary to any of the anger you may have felt that was sincerely expressed, my heart has not hardened. On the contrary, God has protected me from that. So, I am blessed in that I'm still able to feel and to love. Now I just gotta learn how to be loved or rather allow someone to love me, instead of making them fight to break all those barriers I put up to protect myself because of my father abusing, molesting, and raping me.*
You guys call me when you're ready to go out with the old and in with the new.
Love, peace and blessings.
Your sister, your daughter.

This is the first collection of my work through my words. This is years of expressing myself through words, when I had not yet gotten the courage to express myself verbally.

These are my words, my thoughts, my feelings, all of my emotions in print. My life has been very colorful and tumultuous to say the least. But through it all, I am blessed because I am here. I am hoping to one day share my thoughts, words and feelings, with those who can relate, retain and grow. I have come to realize that there are so many little girls, and little boys for that matter that are being harmed every single day. When our voices are stolen at an early age, sometimes we never learn to speak. I am hoping one day that my experiences, my words, and my life can be a stepping stone as well as a mouth opener or mouth piece for others.

This piece gives insight into the sexual abuse that started and continued to take place while I was living with the man born to me as my father. It is also somewhat a summation of my feelings that I allowed myself to divulge to my family, no matter the consequences. It was my intentions to be very explicit and detailed as I want my readers to experience certain feelings and emotions as to understand the seriousness of the matter.

I always try in everything I write to evoke emotion. Within these writings, I have found solace and I have found strength. I can reread my work and feel and see my progress. I write on a daily basis; I'm still learning myself so that in itself may change. I have compiled all of my writings, with the sole purpose of continuing to add more and continue to see and seek my growth. This is only the beginning of my story; there is still so much that needs to be said.

I hope my words could possibly be of help to someone else who may find it hard to speak. At the end of my life, it will be complete, and this will be my gift to myself. The answer to my journey!

This is the birth, a celebration, a representation of ME!

to be continued...

Acknowledgements

There would never be enough words to express my gratitude, nor would there be enough paper to mention every person who has personally touched my life.

To my Lord and Savior. Thank you for gracing me with this opportunity, for opening this door and for trusting me with such a delicate gem.

To my husband, for your patience and love. To my family for supporting me every step of the way. I love you all dearly.

My amazing friends for helping me put this book together, thank you for your sincere friendship.

Lastly, to the brave women in this book, thank you for sharing your stories, for pouring your hearts out and allowing me into such a profound and personal place. For your patience, the late-night texting and infinite emails, I thank you from the depths of my heart.

You have made me brave.
Lauren

Dear Reader

Exhale. You have reached the end. With this last page, we hope you have been encouraged and that your eyes have opened.

Many more women, men and children are suffering daily, due to silence, fear or due to the lack of exposure on the delicate topic of sexual abuse. Our mission is to create awareness and remove the veil blinding the world, causing them to categorize forms of sexual abuse.

Abuse is abuse.

Help us in the fight to keep breaking the silence.

BRAVE

Connect and share your experience personally:
brave.thebook08@gmail.com

Facebook Page:

Brave The Book

Author Instagram:

@lauren.j.covito

Made in the USA
Middletown, DE
13 June 2017